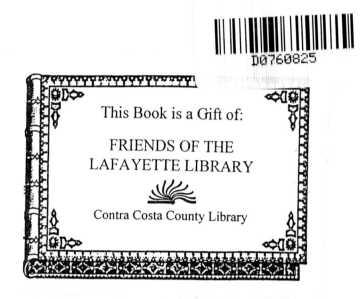

Famous
Dutch Kitchen
Restaurant
COOKBOOK

John and Michelle Morgan's
Famous
Dutch Kitchen
Restaurant
COOKBOOK

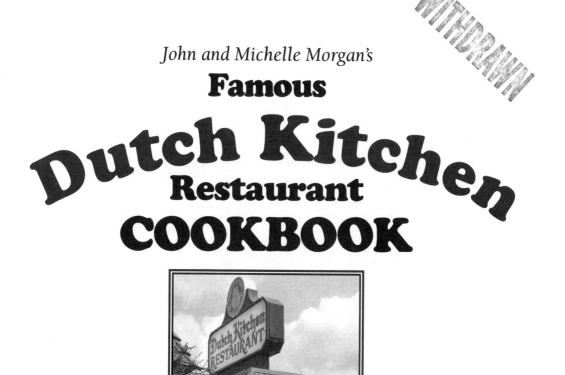

JANE & MICHAEL STERN

With recipes by Tom & Jennifer Levkulic

RUTLEDGE HILL PRESS®

Nashville, Tennessee

Published by Rutledge Hill Press, a Division of Thomas Nelson, Inc., P.O. Box 141000, Nashville, Tennessee, 37214.

Library of Congress Cataloging-in-Publication Data

Stern, Jane.
    The famous Dutch Kitchen restaurant cookbook / Jane & Michael Stern ; with recipes by Tom & Jennifer Levkulic.
        p. cm.
    ISBN 1-4016-0138-3 (Hardcover)
    1. Cookery. 2. dutch Kitchen (Restaurant) I. Stern, Michael, 1946– II. Title.
TX715 .S8443 2004
641.5—dc22   2003024529

Printed in the United States of America

04 05 06 07—5 4 3 2 1

TO JOHN & MICHELLE MORGAN

Your hard work, commitment, and perseverance, along with a dedicated staff and loyal customers, have, made the Dutch Kitchen Restaurant a home away from home for so many.

Contents

Foreword

Thirty-two years ago my parents, John and Michelle Morgan, opened the Dutch Kitchen Restaurant. They had the Silk City Diner Co. diner moved from I-78 outside of Allentown to its present location near I-81 in Frackville, Pennsylvania. What began as a diner that seated sixty grew into a full-service restaurant equipped to handle 180. Although we've tripled our capacity, there are still occasions when customers have to wait for a seat.

Over the years, the Dutch Kitchen Restaurant has truly been a family affair. My parents, sister, Marcia, and myself have all had the privilege of experiencing the busy pace and high energy at the Dutch Kitchen. Now, I am proud to say my husband, Tom, enjoys the restaurant life also. When we met eight years ago, although his background was in the environmental field, he mentioned that he often thought of working in a kitchen. Like me, Tom has a strong family background focused on traditional homemade meals. In 1995 we were married and took over managing the day-to-day business of the Dutch Kitchen Restaurant.

We pride ourselves on being an independent restaurant with original menu ideas stemming from a family that has always felt most comfortable around food—whether it be in our home kitchen or in the kitchen of our restaurant. My great-grandmother Edith Joulwan began this tradition as a baker, chef, and restaurateur specializing in comfort foods with a strong Pennsylvania Dutch and Coal Region influence.

We serve breakfast, lunch, and dinner all day, 363 days of the year. We are closed Thanksgiving and Christmas Day. We like to consider ourselves as a home away from home. Our doors are open to everyone—family members alone for the holidays, travelers stranded in a storm, people celebrating birthdays, graduations, or anniversaries. We like to make everyone feel welcome.

We think the atmosphere can best be described by my mother, Michelle, "It is locals at the diner counter talking to waitresses they have known for twenty-five years or more, a traveler chiming in, jukeboxes on the counter playing oldies, new songs, and holiday favorites. It is seasoned coffee urns, pie cases filled with fresh baked seasonal pies, domes on the counter covering sticky buns and soft sugar cookies. It is the aroma of hearty, substantial food."

Not everyone can make it to the Dutch Kitchen Restaurant to enjoy Pennsylvania Dutch cooking and Frackville hospitality, but now we can come to you through these photographs, stories, and recipes, which we are glad to share. We invite you to experience our eclectic culture, diner delights, and regional fare through this great cookbook made possible by Jane and Michael Stern.

— Jennifer Levkulic

Acknowledgments

Tom and Jen Levkulic and John and Michelle Morgan have been making the Dutch Kitchen a home away from home for so many years, long before we ever thought of collaborating with them on a cookbook. We salute them for their steadfast vision of good cooking. It has been a beacon for us and for countless travelers on the roads of eastern Pennsylvania. And we thank the cooks, waitresses, and hosts at the restaurant who make dining at the counter or table such a personable experience.

We are also deeply indebted to the good people at Rutledge Hill Press who have given us the opportunity to commemorate one of our favorite restaurants in a favorite way: by making its story and its recipes into this book. In particular, we thank publisher Larry Stone, who has shared some great meals with us at America's best tables and whose belief in the concept of a Roadfood cookbook made it happen. We also thank Geoff Stone for his scrupulous editing, Bryan Curtis for his good ideas to spread the word, and Roger Waynick for being the bright spark that ignited this whole idea.

We are especially grateful for the friendship of our comrades at Gourmet magazine, for whom we write a "Roadfood" column. The steady encouragement of Ruth Reichl, James Rodewald, and "Doc" Willoughby are inspiration for us twelve months every year.

We never hit the road without our virtual companions at www.roadfood.com—Steve Rushmore Sr., Stephen Rushmore and Kristin Little, Cindy Keuchle, and Marc Bruno—who constantly fan the flames of appetite and discovery along America's highways and byways.

Thanks also to agent Doe Coover for her tireless work on our behalf, and to Jean Wagner, Jackie Willing, Mary Ann Rudolph, and Ned Schankman for making it possible for us to travel in confidence that all's well at home.

Introduction

In some ways, the Dutch Kitchen is a classic diner, serving three squares a day, from bacon and eggs (and toast from homemade bread) in the morning to a full-course turkey dinner or meatloaf and mashed potatoes for lunch and supper. Beyond those exemplary basics, it is a restaurant that reflects the soul of a region with a rich culinary heritage. Here is the best of Schuylkill County, Pennsylvania—one of this nation's most delicious melting pots.

One hundred years ago, the Southern Coal Field included the most densely populated square mile in the United States. Immigrants from all over Europe, from the north countries and the east as well as the Mediterranean, came here to mine the mineral once known as black gold—anthracite—that fueled the Industrial Revolution. Before they arrived, bringing treasure troves of old-country recipes with them, some half a million settlers from Germany, known as the Pennsylvania Dutch (a misnomer for Deutsch), had already firmly established a culture

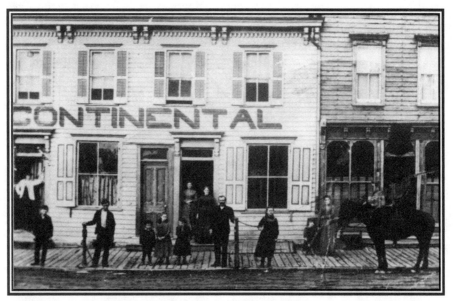

Lehigh Avenue is still Frackville's main street, but the sidewalk is now concrete rather than wood and you'll see far more cars than horses.

Reading Railroad cars take coal from the Great Southern Coal Field, circa 1940.

that included a tradition of eating on the mightiest scale.

In the Dutch Kitchen, customers partake of that diverse history, from tortellini soup and potato-cheese pierogies to Dutchman's red beet pickled eggs and Jewish apple cake. Portions are vast, and the salad bar is a Keystone State cornucopia of relishes, pickled vegetables, sweets and sours, and composed salads. "We have hearty appetites in this part of the country," says the restaurant's long-time cook, Bill Horan. "People work hard for their money, and when they come to dinner, we want to take care of them. They go crazy for the salad bar."

Some of the most nostalgic heartland favorites on the menu are comfort-food dishes originally part of the immigrant repertoire that the rest of America has since forgotten, or perhaps never knew. They include such old-fashioned meals as "city chicken" (skewered pork and veal), mashed potato-topped shepherd's pie, creamed roast turkey on a waffle, double-cut apple-stuffed pork chops, and stuffed cabbage in the winter, at cabbage harvest time.

Despite such colorful edible attractions, a lot of customers come to the Dutch Kitchen primarily because it is so convenient. They may want nothing more than buttermilk pancakes and a good cup of coffee or a hamburger and a wedge of pie. Originally built as an old-fashioned diner, it still has a counter and booths where you can have a lightning-quick meal and be back on the road in a jiffy. In the summer fully half the clientele are travelers looking for a quick meal along the interstate.

Contrary to a fundamental rule of finding Roadfood, which decrees that the quality of a meal is inversely proportional to its proximity to a major highway, this fine diner is just yards from the ramp at Exit 124B off Interstate 81 in Frackville, Pennsylvania. It is a beacon of good eats in the heart of coal country, an easy-off, easy-on restorative for travelers along the big north-south route from Quebec to the Smoky Mountains. It is a restaurant that closes only twice each year—Thanksgiving and Christmas—so that employees can spend the time with their families. The other 363 days locals and loyal travelers count on it for breakfast, lunch, and dinner, or for apple pie and coffee whenever hunger strikes.

Because visitors from the highway are an important part of Dutch Kitchen business, proprietor John Morgan was worried when a Cracker Barrel was constructed five years ago at the same exit off I-81. Would a nationally-known restaurant with a sign posted high above the highway have more appeal to the casual traveler in search of a quick meal than a local eatery? Dutch Kitchen business did, in fact, dip 10 percent the first year the Barrel was open, but it has since risen above where it had been before. Morgan explains why the appearance of the cookie-cutter eatery had so little long-term effect: "There are still plenty of people who want something different than what they've been eating for ten days in a row." The Dutch Kitchen offers not only real food cooked from scratch but also something corporations can't offer, and that's character.

When travel slows in the winter and on weekends, the Dutch Kitchen belongs to the locals. It is Frackville's community gathering place, where people come after funerals, before the Pottsville Winter Carnival, and during town sidewalk sales. Saturday evenings the whole front section of the restaurant is Frackvillians having supper and chatting table to table. Sundays, as after-service church bells ring, parishioners come to the Dutch Kitchen for roast turkey with all

Veteran waitress Barbara Martin serving the people of Frackville.

the fixins, grilled ham steak and scalloped potatoes, or heaps of corned beef and cabbage. Tables are pushed together in the dining room so three generations can all sit together and share Sunday supper in a place where old-timers as well as newcomers feel right at home.

Recently, we received a note from a traveler who described her experience at the Dutch Kitchen as the culinary highlight of a summer vacation. She had been heading south on I-81 with her husband and three children. As sometimes happens on long car trips, everyone was crabby after a day of highway driving, and they were hungry for supper. "The opportunities to dine well are slim along this road, so we didn't have too much hope when we parked next to the Dutch Kitchen. Our plan was to eat fast and get back to driving. But we

slowed down when the food started coming. We all ordered turkey and stuffing and mashed potatoes. My teenage boy went back to the salad bar three times," she said. "Not one of us had a scrap of anything left on our dinner plates. And by the time we got to shoo fly cake and bread pudding—and an atomic banana split for the guys—we were all feeling so good that I wanted to find the cook and kiss her. For us, that meal was Thanksgiving in July."

When entrepreneurs came to John Morgan suggesting he get rich by cloning his restaurant and opening a second, or perhaps a whole string of them, Morgan demurred. "I know I can't be two places at once," he said, "and what makes this restaurant work is the fact that we are here, either I or Tom or Jen [his son-in-law and daughter] and a staff who truly feels that they are part of this place, and it is theirs."

THE DUTCH DINER

If you walk into the Dutch Kitchen through the door near the parking lot, you might never know it started life as a diner. When you enter this way, you are greeted by a hostess and led to a table in a big, wide-open dining room decorated everywhere with Pennsylvania crafts and souvenirs for sale. And here a staff waits on you just as in any other family-style restaurant.

But go in the other door, the one nearer I-81, and behold a pristine mid-century American hash house! Here the décor is all pink and grey enamel with a long, chrome-banded Formica counter attended by a shipshape row of red-upholstered circular stools.

Opposite the counter are Naugahyde booths with flip-card jukeboxes. The ceiling meets the walls in graceful curves and rounded corners; the floor is a tiny-tile pattern of pink and gray. The knee guard at the counter is a natty pattern of larger tiles in the same color scheme. Here is a place to eat that is as crisp, clean, and shiny as the day it first opened its doors in 1959.

For those who appreciate the style of vintage diners, the interior of this one is a doozy, one of Pennsylvania's best. And that's saying a lot, for the state is especially diner-rich, home to some 260 of them, according to Brian Butko and Kevin Patrick in their wonderful book *Diners of Pennsylvania*. Butko and Patrick define *diner* as "a factory-built restaurant transported to its site of operation." By implication, it is a restaurant that can be transported to a new site of operation when the old one becomes untenable. That's exactly what happened to this one. Built by the venerable Silk City Diner Co. of Paterson, New Jersey, it originally was set

up alongside Interstate 78 outside Allentown. Its name was chosen to attract travelers who wanted a taste of Pennsylvania Dutch country.

Business was good . . . until the exit off I-78 was condemned in 1969. The diner closed and sat idle by the highway for a year. John Morgan, a Frackville native whose wife's family had some experience in the restaurant business in Schuylkill County, saw the abandoned dining car as an opportunity. Interstate 81 had been completed in 1967, and it ran right past town. At the time, there were hardly any services at exit ramps between Scranton and Harrisburg, so he bought the diner and moved it to Frackville.

It was in total disrepair," he recalls. "I hired the Parker Brothers to move it, and the move cost six thousand dollars, which was more than I paid for the place! As we came to the outskirts of Frackville, one fellow came up to me and said, 'You aren't putting that thing in town, are you?' It looked that bad. The outside, which had once been shiny steel, was damaged beyond repair by road salt, so once we got it situated, we had to cover it with brick veneer. The interior, however, is bomb-proof. Formica and tile just don't wear out. But it was a real challenge to clean it up. We steam-cleaned everything. When the previous owner had closed, he had just pulled the plug; there was ice cream in the freezer that had sat there for a whole year. There was an inch of moss on everything!

"John should have been a surgeon," says son-in-law Tom Levkulic. "He is so fanatical about cleanliness." After months of cleaning, the Dutch Kitchen opened in its new location on July 14, 1971.

In some ways, the first day was not propitious. Laughing about it now, John remembers, "Within five hours of opening the doors, I had a waitress walk out; we had an electrical short that shut down the lights; and in the darkness, we had a guy walking downstairs to the bathroom who tripped and fell and broke his eyeglasses and his wrist."

The newly-opened Dutch Kitchen survived that first day, and business was good from the beginning. "We were an oasis," John says. "There was one gas station, one motel, and this diner. We sold fifteen-cent coffee and meat loaf dinners for $1.50, and we stayed open for business around the clock. I could see that customers were mostly families looking for meals that were comfortable, nothing exotic. So we stuck to the basics on our menu and have always maintained a family atmosphere."

A new dining room was added in the first year, more than doubling the capacity of the original Silk City diner. And today, while the menu is the same in both the old diner and the spacious dining room, guests have a meaningful choice of environments in which to

This photo of The Valley House hotel was taken in 1892. Today, the Dutch Kitchen occupies the real estate at 405 South Lehigh Avenue.

eat. Big families who come for dinner and groups of coworkers who meet here at lunch choose the new space where tables can be pushed together for parties of eight, ten, twelve, or more. And for many tourists, the vast inventory of crafts for sale all around the tables make this room a shopper's delight. While you dine, you can gaze at speckleware bowls and pitchers, Amish-style quilts, hex signs, tote bags, wall plaques, stuffed animals, bonnets, wind chimes, and welcome signs.

There is no such décor in the old diner, where the pink and grey color scheme, accented by bands of stainless steel and tufted red upholstery, is a complete environment that suffers no extraneous decorative flourishes. It is pure Americana: the great American diner.

· BREAKFAST ·

Farmer's Omelet

Baked Oatmeal

Apple Walnut Pancakes

Griddle Cakes / Hot Cakes / Pancakes

Sticky Buns from Scratch

Short Method Sticky Buns

Sour Cream Coffee Cake

Buttermilk Waffles

Sweet Pumpkin Pancakes

Creamed Chipped Beef

Farmer's Omelet

Here is one good reason always to make extra home-fried potatoes. Reheated leftovers are just right for this mighty omelet, which is a meal for two . . . or for one very hungry farmer.

2	*tablespoons butter*
¼	*cup diced onion*
½	*cup diced green bell pepper*
¼	*cup diced red bell pepper*
1	*cup diced potatoes*
1	*cup diced ham steak*
6	*eggs*
¼	*cup milk*

In a medium-size skillet melt the butter over medium heat. Sauté the onion, green pepper, and red pepper until soft and remove the skillet from the heat. In a separate skillet over medium-high heat add the oil and sauté the potatoes. When potatoes are cooked add the ham steak and brown lightly. Turn the heat to low. In a mixing bowl whisk the eggs and milk until well blended. Add the onion mixture to the egg mixture and pour into the skillet on the stove. When the sides begin to appear dry and look light brown flip the omelet to finish. Cut the omelet in two and serve with toast.

MAKES 2 SERVINGS

Baked Oatmeal

Like the name says, here is a recipe for baked oatmeal. It looks like a cake, but isn't nearly so sweet. It is delicious served warm and topped with cream or whole milk.

2	eggs
1	cup milk
½	cup oil
1	cup firmly packed brown sugar
2	teaspoons baking powder
1	teaspoon salt
3	cups uncooked oatmeal

Preheat the oven to 350°F. In a large bowl combine the eggs, milk, oil, brown sugar, baking powder, and salt. Mix with a wooden spoon and fold in the oatmeal. Pour the oatmeal mixture into a greased 8 x 12-inch baking pan. Bake the oatmeal for about 25 minutes. Serve warm.

MAKES 12 SERVINGS

Apple Walnut Pancakes

For those who like some texture in their pancakes, this recipe adds a nice, fine feel to the batter. As far as we're concerned, real maple syrup is essential here; it sings harmony with the walnuts and apples.

1	cup finely chopped walnuts
2	medium apples
2	to 3 cups pancake batter (see next page)

Peel and core the apples. Chop them into small pieces. Mix the apples and walnuts together. Pour the pancake mix onto a hot buttered skillet. Sprinkle about 2 tablespoons of the apple-walnut mixture on each pancake. When the edges of the pancake are dry, flip it and cook until it's done in the center. Serve the pancakes with butter and maple syrup.

MAKES 2 DOZEN PANCAKES

Griddle Cakes / Hot Cakes / Pancakes

Separating the eggs and prudent handling of the batter make for fluffier pancakes. There is no way to use too much butter when cooking them on a griddle or in a skillet.

1½	cups all-purpose flour
1	teaspoon salt
3	tablespoons sugar
1¾	teaspoons baking powder
2	eggs, separated
1¼	cups milk
1	plus 2 tablespoons melted butter

Sift the flour, salt, sugar, and baking powder. In a separate bowl combine the egg yolks and milk and gently beat. Temper this mixture by adding 1 tablespoon of the butter. Mix and then add the remaining 2 tablespoons butter. Mix well. Add this mixture to the flour mixture, being careful not to overmix. Beat the egg whites until stiff and fold into the pancake mixture. Grill the pancakes on a buttered skillet or griddle over medium heat. Cook until bubbles appear on the surface and the underside is golden brown. Turn the pancake and continue cooking. Serve with butter and maple syrup.

MAKES 2 DOZEN PANCAKES

Sticky Buns from Scratch

From-scratch sticky buns are so good that they are guaranteed not to last as long as it takes to prepare them. The no-shortcuts preparation method hearkens back to the days when the earliest Pennsylvania Dutch settlers found themselves amazed and delighted by the beautiful white flour that was milled from American wheat (as opposed to the dark flour they knew in Europe). No doubt those master bakers were the ones who perfected sticky buns like these—rich and fluffy, enrobed in a sticky, butter-sugar glaze.

1	cup milk
6	plus 2 tablespoons granulated sugar
1	teaspoon salt
1	envelope active dry yeast
½	cup warm water
5	plus ¼ cups all-purpose flour
4	plus 3 plus 1 tablespoons butter, softened (1 stick total)
1	egg
⅔	cup firmly packed light brown sugar
½	plus 1 teaspoons ground cinnamon
½	cup light corn syrup
½	cup walnuts, chopped

In a small saucepan heat the milk over medium-low heat. Stir 6 tablespoons of the granulated sugar and the salt into the milk until dissolved. Remove the milk from the heat and set it aside to cool. Sprinkle the yeast over the warm water and set it aside to proof. Put 5 cups of the flour into a large bowl and make a well in the center. When the milk is cool pour it into the center of the flour. Add the yeast mixture, 4 tablespoons of the butter, and the egg. Stir with a wooden spoon until a soft dough forms. Sprinkle a pastry mat or the counter top with the remaining ¼ cup flour. Place the dough on the floured surface and knead until smooth. Oil a large bowl. Place the dough in the bowl, turning it until it is coated with oil. Cover the bowl with a towel and set it aside in a warm place until the dough doubles in size, about 50 minutes. In a small bowl combine 3 tablespoons of the butter, the brown sugar, ½ teaspoon of the cinnamon, and corn syrup. Pour the brown sugar mixture into a 13 x 9 x 2-inch baking pan. Sprinkle the walnuts over the sugar mixture. Combine the remaining 1 teaspoon cinnamon with the remaining 2 tablespoons granulated sugar. Divide the dough in half and roll out each half to make a 12-inch square. Spread half of the remaining 1 tablespoon butter and sprinkle half the cinnamon-sugar on each square of dough. Roll up each square like a jelly roll and cut into 6 pieces. Place the pieces in the pan, swirl-side up. Cover the pan with a towel and set aside in a warm place to let the buns rise to double in size, about 1 hour.

When ready to bake, preheat the oven to 350°F. Bake the sticky buns until they are nicely brown, about 25 minutes. Remove them from the oven and let them sit for 5 minutes. Then turn the pan upside down onto a tray to remove the buns while still hot.

MAKES 12 SERVINGS

Short Method Sticky Buns

The Levkulics' eight-year-old nephew, John Dylan, loves these sticky buns so much that he once ate an entire 9 x 13-inch pan of them while the family was waiting for out-of-town guests to arrive. "When we realized what had happened, we all just looked at each other with an expression of 'holy cow!'" Tom laughs.

2   *cups raisins*

2   *frozen bread loaves, thawed but not risen*

½   *cup (1 stick) butter*

1   *cup firmly packed brown sugar*

1   *(4½-ounce) box vanilla pudding (not instant; do not follow box directions)*

2   *tablespoons milk*

½   *teaspoon ground cinnamon*

Grease a 9 x 13-inch baking pan. Sprinkle the raisins into the pan. Cut 1 loaf of bread into 2-inch squares and place the pieces on top of the raisins. In a small saucepan melt the butter over medium heat. Add the brown sugar and stir until dissolved. Add the pudding, milk, and cinnamon. Cook for a few minutes until heated through. Pour the pudding mixture over the bread. Cut the remaining loaf of bread into 2-inch squares. Place the bread pieces on top of the pudding mixture. Let the bread sit at room temperature for 2½ to 3 hours to rise. When risen, preheat the oven to 325°F. Bake the sticky buns for 30 minutes. When they are done, remove them from the oven and let them sit for 5 minutes. Turn the pan upside down onto a tray to remove the sticky buns while still hot.

MAKES 12 SERVINGS

Variation: Locals enjoy their sticky buns buttered and grilled for one minute on each side to ensure hot delivery.

14

Sour Cream Coffee Cake

Perfect in the morning with coffee as a breakfast treat or at the end of the day as a snack, this is a cake just like Mom would make.

½	cup (1 stick) butter
1	plus ½ cups sugar
2	eggs, well beaten
2	cups cake flour
1	teaspoon baking powder
1	teaspoon baking soda
¼	teaspoon salt
1	cup sour cream
1	teaspoon vanilla extract
½	cup chopped walnuts
1	teaspoon ground cinnamon

Preheat the oven to 350°F. Cream the butter, 1 cup of the sugar, and the eggs together in a bowl. Sift together the cake flour, baking powder, baking soda, and salt in a separate bowl. Add the flour mixture to the butter mixture. Add the sour cream and vanilla and mix well. In a separate bowl mix the nuts, the remaining ½ cup sugar, and cinnamon. Pour half the batter into a greased tube pan. Sprinkle half the walnuts on top. Pour the remaining batter on top and finish by sprinkling the remaining walnuts on top. Bake for 45 minutes or until a cake tester comes out clean.

MAKES 12 SERVINGS

Buttermilk Waffles

In the kitchens of Pennsylvania Dutch cooks, waffles aren't just for breakfast. They serve as a bed for creamed meats or vegetables at lunch and supper, too. While this recipe works in the larger Belgian-style waffle iron, we think you'll get a better, crisper waffle in the old-fashioned small-tread iron.

2	cups all-purpose flour
¼	teaspoon baking soda
1⅓	teaspoons baking powder
1	tablespoon sugar
½	teaspoon salt
2	eggs, separated
1¾	cups buttermilk
6	tablespoons melted butter

Sift the flour, baking soda, baking powder, sugar, and salt together. In a separate bowl beat the egg yolks with the buttermilk. Slowly add the melted butter by adding 1 tablespoon, mixing well, and then adding the remaining melted butter. Add the milk mixture to the flour mixture, being careful not to overmix. In a separate bowl beat the egg whites until stiff and fold them into the waffle batter. Grease the waffle iron if necessary. Serve the waffles with butter and maple syrup.

MAKES 6 WAFFLES

Variation: For a great lunch or dinner idea, top a freshly baked waffle with chunks of turkey, mixed vegetables, and turkey gravy.

Sweet Pumpkin Pancakes

Pumpkin pancakes are a natural way to start a brisk autumn day, but there is no reason they cannot be enjoyed year around . . . and for lunch as well as breakfast.

2	cups pancake batter (see page 11)
2	tablespoons brown sugar
2	teaspoons ground cinnamon
1	teaspoon allspice
1	teaspoon vanilla extract
1½	cups evaporated milk
½	cup pumpkin purée
2	tablespoon vegetable oil
2	eggs, beaten

Preheat a griddle to 350°F. In a medium-size mixing bowl, combine the pancake batter, brown sugar, cinnamon, and allspice and blend well. In a separate bowl combine the vanilla, evaporated milk, pumpkin purée, vegetable oil, and eggs. Add the wet ingredients to the dry ingredients and gently fold together making sure not to overbeat. Grease the hot griddle with butter or nonstick spray and pour ¼ cup batter onto it, grilling the pumpkin cakes on both sides until golden brown. Serve with butter and maple syrup.

MAKES 2 DOZEN PANCAKES

Creamed Chipped Beef

Military men know this dish as S.O.S. (Stuff on a Shingle). Bad creamed chipped beef is something awful indeed. But good "stuff," made fresh with plenty of real butter, is one luxurious way to start the day.

½   cup (1 stick) butter

½   pound dried beef, very thinly sliced, chipped

½   cup all-purpose flour

8   cups half-and-half

6   slices toast

While melting the butter in a large saucepan, dredge the dried beef in the flour, reserving the leftover flour for later. Add the dried beef to the melted butter and cook until the beef is slightly brown. Sprinkle any leftover flour over the beef and stir. Slowly add the half-and-half and cook over low heat, always stirring to prevent burning. Cook until smooth and thick. Ladle over the toast and serve.

MAKES 6 SERVINGS

BREADS &
MUFFINS

Zucchini Bread

Poppy Seed Bread

Irish Soda Bread

Cornbread

Peach Quick Bread

Bran Muffins

Cranberry-Nut Muffins

Berry Special Muffins

Peanut Butter Raisin Muffins

Zucchini Bread

Zucchini is one of nature's wonders. From a vegetable that looks like a cucumber, cooks make some of the most rich and delicious baked goods. Like good banana bread, this loaf has a gentle fruity taste and moist texture.

3½	cups all-purpose flour
1	teaspoon salt
1	teaspoon baking powder
1	teaspoon baking soda
½	teaspoon ground cinnamon
½	teaspoon ground nutmeg
3	cups grated zucchini
1	cup raisins
4	eggs, well beaten
2	cups sugar
1	cup canola oil
1	teaspoon vanilla extract

Preheat the oven to 350°F. In a large bowl mix together the flour, salt, baking powder, baking soda, cinnamon, and nutmeg. Add the zucchini, raisins, eggs, sugar, oil, and vanilla and mix well. Pour the batter into 2 greased and floured loaf pans. Bake the bread for 30 minutes.

MAKES 2 LOAVES

Poppy Seed Bread

When Jennifer was growing up, her mother, Michelle, used this recipe to make poppy seed bread. She advises always to look in the mirror after eating a piece. The poppy seeds have a habit of getting stuck between your teeth.

2	eggs
1⅛	cups sugar
1	cup evaporated milk
1	cup canola oil
2	cups all-purpose flour
2	teaspoons baking powder
½	teaspoon salt
¼	cup poppy seeds

Preheat the oven to 350°F. Beat the eggs, sugar, milk, and oil together in a bowl. Add the flour, baking powder, salt, and poppy seeds. Mix well and pour the batter into a greased 9 x 5-inch pan. Bake the bread for 1 hour.

MAKES 12 SERVINGS

Irish Soda Bread

In the ethnic smorgasbord that is Schuylkill County, there are plenty of Irishmen; and around St. Patrick's Day, you can be sure corned beef and cabbage will be on the Dutch Kitchen menu. Irish soda bread is a natural companion.

2	cups all-purpose flour
¼	cup oats
¾	teaspoon baking soda
½	teaspoon kosher salt
1	tablespoon sugar
6	tablespoons chilled butter
⅔	cup vanilla yogurt
½	cup dark raisins
½	cup golden raisins
1	tablespoon milk

Preheat the oven to 350°F. In a large mixing bowl combine the flour, oats, baking soda, kosher salt, and sugar; mix well. Cut in the chilled butter until the mixture is crumb-like. Gradually add the yogurt and raisins. Gently knead the dough into a round loaf. Place the dough onto a greased baking sheet. Cut an *X* across the top of the loaf and brush the top with milk. Bake the dough for 40 to 50 minutes or until golden brown.

MAKES 1 LOAF, 10 TO 12 SLICES

Cornbread

Tender and distinctively sweet, this fine cornbread verges on being cake. But it's a terrific companion to any hot meal, especially welcome alongside a bowl of chili or ham and cabbage stew.

1	cup cornmeal
2	cups all-purpose flour
1	cup sugar
8	teaspoons baking powder
2	eggs, well beaten
⅔	cup canola oil
2	cups milk

Preheat the oven to 375°F. Mix the cornmeal, flour, sugar, and baking powder together in a large bowl. In a separate bowl combine the eggs with the oil and milk. Add the wet mixture to the dry mixture. Do not overmix. Pour the batter into a greased and floured 9 x 13-inch pan and bake for 40 minutes.

MAKES 12 SERVINGS

Peach Quick Bread

In the summertime, when grower Steve Harding's peaches are ripe and ready to eat, the Dutch Kitchen offers this quick bread infused with the fresh fruit's flavor.

BREAD:

2½   cups all-purpose flour

¾   cup sugar

1   tablespoon baking powder

½   teaspoon salt

¼   teaspoon ground nutmeg

1   tablespoon fresh lemon juice

⅓   cup milk

2   eggs, well beaten

2   teaspoons vanilla extract

1½   cups peeled and sliced fresh peaches

TOPPING:

¼   cup all-purpose flour

2   tablespoons brown sugar

2   tablespoons cold butter

Preheat the oven to 350°F. For the bread, mix together the flour, sugar, baking powder, salt, and nutmeg in a large bowl. In a separate bowl, mix together the lemon juice, milk, eggs, and vanilla. Add the wet mixture to the dry mixture. Do not overmix. Fold in the peaches. Pour the batter into a greased and floured loaf pan.

For the topping, combine the flour, brown sugar, and butter in a bowl. Crumble the mixture together with your hands. Sprinkle the crumbled mixture over the top of the bread batter. Bake the bread for 50 minutes.

MAKES 12 SERVINGS

Bran Muffins

This is a morning favorite at the Dutch Kitchen, both in the dining room and at the counter in the old diner. This bran muffin is very moist but not sugary—a dandy companion for coffee.

3½	cups bran flakes
1½	cups sugar
2½	cups all-purpose flour
2½	teaspoons baking soda
1	teaspoon salt
2	eggs, well beaten
½	cup canola oil
2	cups buttermilk

Preheat the oven to 375°F. In a large bowl mix together the bran flakes, sugar, flour, baking soda, salt, eggs, oil, and buttermilk. Let the batter rest for 40 minutes before pouring it into greased and floured muffin pans. Bake the muffins for 25 minutes.

MAKES 2 DOZEN MUFFINS

Famous Dutch Kitchen Restaurant Cookbook

Cranberry-Nut Muffins

Cranberry-nut muffins are a holiday staple. You'll find bunches of them piled up every morning on the counter of the Dutch Kitchen's 1950s Silk City diner car.

2	cups all-purpose flour
1	cup sugar
1½	teaspoons baking powder
1	teaspoon salt
½	teaspoon baking soda
¼	cup (½ stick) margarine
1	egg, well beaten
¾	cup orange juice
1	tablespoon orange zest
1½	cups chopped fresh cranberries
1	cup chopped walnuts

Preheat the oven to 350°F. In a large bowl mix together the flour, sugar, baking powder, salt, and baking soda. Cut the margarine into the dry mixture until crumbs form. In a small bowl whisk together the egg, orange juice, and orange zest. Add the egg mixture to the dry mixture, stirring until combined. Fold in the cranberries and walnuts. Pour the batter into a greased and floured muffin pan. Bake the muffins for 20 minutes.

MAKES 12 MUFFINS

Berry Special Muffins

Jennifer's Nana, Lois, gave her this recipe, which should be made in the summertime when local blueberries are full-flavored.

½	cup vanilla yogurt
¼	cup milk
⅓	cup firmly packed dark brown sugar
¼	cup canola oil
1	egg
1¾	cups all-purpose flour
1	tablespoon baking powder
¼	teaspoon salt
¼	teaspoon baking soda
1	cup blueberries
	Granulated sugar

Preheat the oven to 400°F. Combine the yogurt, milk, brown sugar, canola oil, and egg in a mixing bowl. In a separate bowl stir together the flour, baking powder, salt, and baking soda. Gently mix the wet mixture with the dry mixture until just combined. Fold in the berries. Pour the batter into a greased muffin pan. Sprinkle the granulated sugar on top and bake for 25 minutes.

MAKES 1 DOZEN MUFFINS

Peanut Butter Raisin Muffins

Rich, chunky, and moist, these muffins are a joy to eat for breakfast or a full-size snack any time of day.

1	pound raisins
2½	plus ¼ cups warm water
1	pound brown sugar
½	pound (2 sticks) butter
½	cup peanut butter
2	teaspoons baking soda
1	cup chopped peanuts
4	cups all-purpose flour
2	teaspoons ground cinnamon
1	teaspoon ground nutmeg
1	cup applesauce

Preheat the oven to 350°F. Combine the raisins and 2½ cups of the water in a saucepan and cook on medium heat for 10 minutes. Add the brown sugar, butter, and peanut butter and mix well. Remove from the heat and let cool. In a small bowl dissolve the baking soda in the remaining ¼ cup water and add to the cooled raisin mixture. Add the peanuts, flour, cinnamon, nutmeg, and applesauce. Mix to combine. Do not overmix. Pour the batter into greased muffin pans. Bake for 30 minutes or until an inserted knife comes out clean.

MAKES 2 DOZEN MUFFINS

FRACKVILLE, PA

Coal was once as good as gold. The earth underneath Frackville and the surrounding towns of Pottsville and Tamaqua is veined with anthracite of the great Southern Coal Field of eastern Pennsylvania. The discovery and mining of this lode in the mid- nineteenth century attracted waves of immigrants to Schuylkill County.

In 1833, before the coal boom, Daniel Frack settled in the town of St. Clair (just a few miles south of where Frackville is today), and while Frack himself was not in the coal business, his St. Clair hostelry and subsequent real estate investments made him a wealthy man. In the years before the Civil War, Frack moved north to what was then known as Girard Place and made some of his land there available as building lots. After the War, as the coal industry burgeoned and new settlers came to work the mines, Frack's properties grew all the more valuable. First settled in 1854, the Borough of Frackville, population 200 freeholders (not counting women, as they couldn't yet vote), was granted a government charter in America's centennial year, 1876.

It seems right that Frackville was formally put on the map in 1876,

for it is an extraordinarily patriotic place. During an hour's breakfast one morning in the old diner part of the Dutch Kitchen, we heard Lee Greenwood's "God Bless the USA" played three times on the jukebox. "This town has a lot of pride and spirit," says owner John Morgan. "We have so many service-oriented churches here, and the community has always taken great pride in its citizens who have served in the armed forces. In Frackville, people wave the flag."

Morgan means that quite literally. Drive around Frackville and you'll be astonished at how many American flags you see. They are hung on front porches along the residential streets and from businesses along Lehigh Avenue, the main drag. In addition to the stars and stripes, homes sport yellow ribbons in support of those serving overseas,

The Reading Railroad cars are loaded with anthracite coal.

statuettes of Uncle Sam by the front door, and welcome signs that announce *God Bless America.* "You should have been here in 1976," John Morgan says. "It was our centennial and the nation's bicentennial. The celebration that year was incredible."

Perhaps some of that patriotism goes back to the way immigrants felt when they arrived here. Other than the Statue of Liberty herself, few attractions of the new world were more magnetic for the people of the old world than the mines. Digging minerals and coal from the earth promised wealth for a few but at least gave steady wages for the many, and so they came to where the work was. Schuylkill County genealogies trace local founding families back to Germany, Scotland, Ireland, England, Wales, France, Greece, Lithuania, Poland, and Slovakia.

Coal was the lifeblood of the region. Coal companies were bigger than the government. They owned the land and the minerals in it; they owned the "company store" where workers shopped; and they owned the homes in which people lived. "Coal mining was a very hard life," one Schuylkill County old-timer reminisced. "But I have never met a coal miner who didn't love his job. My grandfather began working in the coal mines at age six (he lied about his age). At age eighty-five, his eyes filled with tears when he related some of his favorite stories. He would have been happy to go back into the mines, even at age eighty-five. The coal miner and his family were a hardy lot."

Coal was so much a part of life that locals like to recall the many uses it had other than as heat for homes and as a source of income. One person remembered that his grandmother cooked with it; the town used coal ashes to "sand" roads in winter; and coal itself was especially fascinating to neighborhood children. One of them wrote, "Racing onto someone's porch to watch the coal delivery [and] coal going down the chute and into the bin … that was entertainment for all us kids on the block back in the 1940s and 1950s."

One of the most valuable bequests of workers from around the world to this coalfield country was the recipes they and their families brought

This 1930s Frackville eatery was known as the Charles Kirelawich Café. It's a good example of the diverse ethnic heritage of the community.

with them. This is apparent in Frackville throughout the year in such community events as pierogi festivals and bleenie weekends (pierogies are Polish dumplings; bleenies are Eastern European potato pancakes), and on Lehigh Avenue at the Olde World Cheesecake Company where the cheesecakes, coffee cakes, tarts, and cookies reveal confectionery traditions that go back to the community's ancestral homelands. Immigrants from Germany established Yuengling Brewery in 1829 down the road in Pottsville; it is now the nation's oldest brewery.

While the Dutch Kitchen is very much a meat-and-potatoes diner, its cooking also mirrors the diverse ethnic heritage of the community. Of course, there is Dutch (Deutsch) food including pot pies and fresh Lancaster County sausage, but there is also Kowalonek's kielbasa, a local brand so treasured by those who live here that around the holidays the line to get some stretches half a block out the butcher shop. Tom Levkulic, himself of Lithuanian descent, makes a fabulous soup of smoked Polish kielbasa and Italian tortellini—a literal melting pot—and his holupki (stuffed cabbage) is a wintertime dish loved by regulars.

One of the curious ethnic legacies on the Dutch Kitchen menu is Jewish apple cake. This is a dense, moist coffee cake laced with soft apple slivers that makes a great pastry with coffee at breakfast, or a mid-afternoon snack, or dessert after a big meal. John Morgan has been known to bake bunches of Jewish apple cakes and bring them as a good will gesture to local funeral directors and others in town who sent him business. Curiously, neither John Morgan nor Tom and Jennifer Levkulic can explain why it is called *Jewish* apple cake. As far as they know, it is not Jewish, nor is it unique to the Dutch Kitchen. We found it served at the local bakery, too. Tom remembers it as part of his own Lithuanian mother's repertoire from his growing-up years around here. And John says it got on the Dutch Kitchen menu as a recipe from his wife's grandmother, Edith Joulwan.

"Was she Jewish?" we ask, looking for an explanation of the cake's name.

"No," John answers. "She was Lebanese."

DRESSINGS, SAUCES & SPREADS

Tomato Sauce

Cold Horseradish Sauce

Hot Horseradish Sauce

Raisin Sauce

Cheese Sauce

BBQ Sauce

Lemony Dill Sauce

Mayonnaise

Apple Butter

Peanut Butter with Honey

Hot Bacon Dressing

1000 Island Dressing

Blue Cheese Dressing

Tomato Sauce

Italian-American food is a mighty presence throughout the coal belt, where so many Italians came to work in the mines. From Old Forge-style pizza around Scranton to pepperoni rolls in West Virginia, the regional cuisine is rich with Old Country flavor. This is the Dutch Kitchen's "gravy," a.k.a. tomato sauce, suitable for any kind of pasta.

2	cups diced onions
1	tablespoon minced garlic
½	cup olive oil
1	(24-ounce) can crushed tomatoes
1	(8-ounce) can tomato paste
½	cup sugar
1	teaspoon salt
1	teaspoon dried basil
1	teaspoon dried oregano
	Black pepper
¼	teaspoon crushed red pepper
2	cups water

Sauté the onions and garlic in the olive oil. Add the crushed tomatoes, tomato paste, sugar, salt, basil, oregano, black pepper to taste, and crushed red pepper. Add the water and bring the sauce to a boil. Turn down the heat and allow the sauce to simmer for about 2 hours.

MAKES 4 CUPS

Cold Horseradish Sauce

Think of this with cool, sliced beef, or on the side of shellfish or salmon.

1	cup mayonnaise
3	tablespoons prepared horseradish
2	tablespoons whipping cream
1	teaspoon sugar
1	teaspoon dry mustard
1	tablespoon white vinegar

In a medium mixing bowl combine the mayonnaise, horseradish, whipping cream, sugar, dry mustard, and vinegar. Mix well.

MAKES 1¼ CUP

Hot Horseradish Sauce

When serving locally-made kielbasa, hot horseradish sauce is a preferred condiment. It's also great on the side with roast beef or pot roast.

1	tablespoon butter
1	teaspoon all-purpose flour
½	teaspoon salt
⅛	teaspoon paprika
¼	cup heavy whipping cream
1	egg yolk, slightly beaten
½	cup grated horseradish root

Melt the butter in a saucepan. Stir in the flour, salt, and paprika and cook until the mixture bubbles. Gradually add the cream and bring to a boil, stirring constantly. Cook 2 minutes longer. Stir several teaspoons of the mixture into the egg yolk and then mix into the sauce. Cook and stir 2 minutes longer. Blend in the horseradish. Heat thoroughly and serve with roast beef, kielbasa, or many sandwiches.

MAKES ¼ CUP

Raisin Sauce

This is ham's best friend. On Easter Sunday especially, but any day when you crave the Dutch Kitchen's traditional ham dinner, this raisin sauce sings sweet harmony.

2	*cups (4 sticks) butter*
1	*cup all-purpose flour*
2	*cups beef stock*
2	*cups apple juice*
2	*cups raisins*
1	*tablespoon lemon juice*
1	*teaspoon crushed cloves*
½	*cup firmly packed brown sugar*

In a large saucepan on low heat melt the butter. With a wire whisk add the flour and mix well. Add the beef stock, apple juice, raisins, lemon juice, cloves, and brown sugar. Cook over low heat until thickened, about 20 minutes. Serve on top of baked ham.

MAKES 6 CUPS

Cheese Sauce

Here is a basic cheese sauce to serve warm over baked fish or chicken. It's also nice atop such vegetables as cauliflower or broccoli.

1	cup (2 sticks) butter
1	cup all-purpose flour
2	cups half-and-half
1	pound grated sharp cheese

In a medium saucepan over low heat melt the butter and mix in the flour with a wire whisk. Add the half-and-half and cook on low heat, stirring frequently. Do not allow to boil. Add the grated cheese and continue stirring until well blended. Use for a topping on fish or chicken.

MAKES 4 CUPS

BBQ Sauce

For slathering on meats as they cook or as a warm dip-and-dunk on a plate along with roasted chicken wings, or sweet sausage, this sauce is a quick and efficient way to add zest to a meal.

½	cup vegetable oil
1	cup diced onion
1	cup diced green bell pepper
4	cups ketchup
½	cup apple cider vinegar
½	cup firmly packed light brown sugar
2	tablespoons liquid smoke
¼	cup pickle relish

Heat the vegetable oil in a saucepan over medium heat. Sauté the onion and green pepper. Add the ketchup, vinegar, brown sugar, liquid smoke, and pickle relish. Slowly cook the sauce on medium heat until the mixture reaches a boil. Remove from the heat and serve warm.

MAKES 4 CUPS

Lemony Dill Sauce

Here's a handy sauce that goes well on just about any kind of baked or broiled fish. Think of it also as gilt for simple baked chicken.

½	cup margarine
1	cup mayonnaise
1	egg
2	tablespoons lemon juice
2	tablespoons water
1	tablespoon sugar
1	tablespoon chicken base
½	teaspoon dried dill weed

In a saucepan over low heat, melt the margarine and add the mayonnaise, egg, lemon juice, water, sugar, chicken base, and dill weed. Cook just until blended. Serve warm over the seafood of your choice.

MAKES 3 CUPS

Mayonnaise

Hellman's is an honored name around our house, and while we certainly wouldn't advise anyone always to blend his or her own mayonnaise, there are special occasions when the extras make all the difference.

2	egg yolks, beaten	½	teaspoon dry mustard
1	teaspoon salt	4	tablespoons lemon juice
¼	teaspoon paprika	2	cups vegetable oil
2	teaspoons sugar		

Place the egg yolks in a large bowl. In a separate bowl mix together the salt, paprika, sugar, and dry mustard. Add the lemon juice to moisten. Add this mixture to the egg yolks. Mix well and add the oil by drops at first, finishing more quickly. Beat vigorously until the mixture becomes smooth and thick.

MAKES 3 CUPS

Apple Butter

We are fortunate to have three good farm stands. Produce is sold in a variety of quart, peck, and bushel baskets. Four quarts of apples is equal to half a peck or 32 to 40 medium-size apples. When made into apple butter, they are reduced to about three quarts of apples."

Use this apple butter as a relish on your salad plate or alongside dinner, or spread it on savory or sweet bread. We like it in the morning on pancakes and French toast.

8	cups apple cider	½	cup honey
4	quarts (32 to 40 medium) apples	1½	cups dark corn syrup
2	cups sugar	1	teaspoon ground cinnamon

Boil the cider in a large stockpot until it is reduced by half. Peel, core, and slice the apples into thin slices. Add the apples to the cider and cook slowly on low heat until the mixture begins to thicken. Stir frequently. Add the sugar, honey, corn syrup, and cinnamon. Continue to cook until the apple butter is of good spreading consistency.

MAKES ABOUT 3 QUARTS

Peanut Butter with Honey

You'll find peanut butter with honey, made with Tom's honey, on the Dutch Kitchen salad bar. Regular customers know to spread it on the good, dark rye bread that is freshly baked at Frackville's own New York Bakery.

1	*cup wildflower honey*
2	*cups peanut butter*

With an electric mixer blend the honey and peanut butter on high speed. Serve at room temperature.

MAKES 3 CUPS

Hot Bacon Dressing

Dandelion greens topped with hot bacon dressing is a Pennsylvania Dutch mainstay. When dandelion greens are not in season, a nice tossed salad will do. Many people like this salad before a serving of turkey potpie.

4	slices bacon
¼	cup white vinegar
½	cup sugar
¼	cup water
2	eggs, well beaten

In a small frying pan cook the bacon until crisp. Drain the bacon on paper towels and reserve the bacon fat from the frying pan. When the bacon has cooled, chop it. Combine the bacon fat, vinegar, sugar, water, and eggs in a medium saucepan and cook on medium heat. Add the bacon. Serve the dressing warm over the salad of your choice.

MAKES 1¼ CUPS

1000 Island Dressing

The name has nothing to do with the fact that this dressing resembles a thousand pickle atolls in a smooth pink sea. The name refers to its birthplace, a stretch of the St. Lawrence River called the Thousand Islands, where the dressing was first served at the Herald Hotel a century ago.

4	cups mayonnaise	½	cup sweet pickle juice, drained from pickle relish
2	cups ketchup		
1	cup diced celery	¼	teaspoon salt
¼	cup pickle relish	¼	teaspoon black pepper
¼	cup water	¼	cup sugar

In a large mixing bowl combine the mayonnaise, ketchup, celery, pickle relish, water, pickle juice, salt, pepper, and sugar. Mix well with a wooden spoon.

MAKES 6 CUPS

Blue Cheese Dressing

This is a smooth, creamy blue cheese dressing. Its flavor is dependent primarily on the quality of cheese used. We love it especially with Maytag blue cheese from Iowa.

1	cup mayonnaise
2	cups sour cream
½	tablespoon garlic salt
½	teaspoon ground white pepper
1	cup blue cheese crumbles

In a medium mixing bowl combine the mayonnaise, sour cream, garlic salt, and white pepper and mix well. Add the blue cheese and mix.

MAKES 4 CUPS

· SALAD BAR · SPECIALS

Pepper Relish

Mild Pepper Slaw

Hot Pepper Slaw

Coleslaw

Five-Cup Salad

Fresh Corn Pudding

Brown Sugar Pears

Cucumbers in Cream Dressing

Sweet & Sour Cucumber Salad

Pickled Eggs

Three-Bean Salad

Potato Salad

Hot Potato Salad

Red Beet Salad

Applesauce Salad

Pepper Relish

This is a colorful condiment that looks great on the side of just about any hot meal. Its zest pairs well with creamy cottage cheese on a salad plate.

12	sweet red peppers
12	sweet green peppers
12	medium onions
1	gallon (16 cups) boiling water
2	cups sugar
2	tablespoons celery salt
1	quart (4 cups) apple cider vinegar
2	tablespoons mustard seed
2	tablespoons salt

Finely chop the peppers and onions in a food processor. Put them in a large stockpot and cover them with the boiling water. Let them stand for 5 to 10 minutes before draining. In a saucepan combine the sugar, celery salt, vinegar, mustard seed, and salt and bring to a boil. Add the chopped peppers and onions and boil for 10 minutes. Pour the relish into jars and seal.

MAKES ABOUT 6 QUARTS

Mild Pepper Slaw

Finely shredded pepper slaw is an essential on the salad bar and an especially good companion for the Dutch Kitchen's beer-batter haddock.

1	cup water	2	medium green bell peppers, chopped
½	cup sugar		
½	teaspoon salt	2	tablespoons celery seeds
1	cup cider vinegar	1	medium head cabbage, finely shredded
1	medium red bell pepper, chopped		

Combine the water, sugar, salt, and vinegar. In a seperate bowl combine the peppers, celery seeds, and cabbage and toss. Add the vinegar mixture to the pepper mixture, mix well, and let stand in a cool place for several hours before serving.

MAKES 10 SERVINGS

Hot Pepper Slaw

For those who like their slaw hot, this recipe adds a good measure of horseradish. The heat of horseradish can vary tremendously and also changes over time, so taste it first before adding any.

1	small head cabbage	½	cup sugar
1	small green bell pepper	1	teaspoon salt
1	cup cider vinegar	2	teaspoons celery seed
1	cup water	1	tablespoon horseradish

Shred the cabbage and green pepper. In a large mixing bowl combine the cabbage, pepper, vinegar, water, sugar, salt, celery seed, and horseradish. Thoroughly mix the slaw with your hands before serving.

MAKES 8 SERVINGS

Coleslaw

Not surprisingly, the cooks of Pennsylvania Dutch country have devised dozens of different kinds of coleslaw: hot, sweet, tangy, creamy. This one from the Dutch Kitchen salad bar is a classic: creamy with vinegar sass and bright orange threads of carrot.

1	*medium head cabbage*
2	*cups mayonnaise*
½	*cup sugar*
2	*cups vinegar*
2	*cups shredded carrots*

Shred the cabbage. In a large mixing bowl combine the mayonnaise, sugar, vinegar, and carrots. Add the cabbage and mix well. Refrigerate the coleslaw for 1 hour before serving.

MAKES 8 SERVINGS

Five-Cup Salad

No church supper or heartland salad bar is complete without at least one version of this oh-so-easy sweet salad. At the Dutch Kitchen you'll always find it around holiday time, or other times, as Tom says, "just because we love it."

1	(16-ounce) bag mini marshmallows
1	(16-ounce) can crushed pineapple
1	(14-ounce) can mandarin oranges
1	(16-ounce) bag shredded coconut
1	pint sour cream

In a large bowl add the marshmallows, pineapple, mandarin oranges, coconut, and sour cream. Mix the salad gently and serve it chilled.

MAKES 8 SERVINGS

Fresh Corn Pudding

Because it grows abundantly in the region and because it can be stored well, corn is a staple ingredient of many wonderful Lancaster County recipes.

¼	cup chopped celery	¼	teaspoon paprika
¼	cup chopped onion	1	cup milk
¼	cup (½ stick) butter	2¼	cups fresh corn kernels
2	tablespoons all-purpose flour	2	tablespoons chopped parsley
1	teaspoon salt	2	eggs, well beaten

Preheat the oven to 350°F. Cook the celery and onion in the butter in a skillet over medium heat until soft. Mix the flour, salt, and paprika in a bowl and add to the celery and onion in the skillet. Heat until bubbly. Gradually add the milk, stirring constantly. Bring rapidly to a boil, cook, and stir 2 minutes longer. Mix in the corn and parsley. Fold in the beaten eggs. Turn the mixture into a buttered, shallow, 1½-quart baking dish. Bake the pudding for 35 minutes or until a butter knife comes out clean. To serve, cut it into squares.

MAKES 6 SERVINGS

Brown Sugar Pears

Spiced pears are one of the principal elements of the long-established catalog of "seven sweets and seven sours." While fresh Seckel pears can be used for texture, by the time the pears are smothered in the sweet, spicy syrup there's little flavor difference between fresh and canned.

2	*pounds firmly packed brown sugar*
3	*tablespoons vinegar*
3	*teaspoons cloves*
3	*teaspoons ground cinnamon*
1	*(16-ounce) can pears, drained*

Cook the brown sugar, vinegar, cloves, and cinnamon in a stockpot on medium heat until thick, stirring occasionally. Pour the mixture over the pears and serve.

MAKES 6 SERVINGS

Cucumbers in Cream Dressing

While the majority of cucumbers that come into the Pennsylvania Dutch kitchen get pickled, here's a smooth, mellow alternative that is particularly welcome when summer's cukes are fresh.

1	*large cucumber*
1	*teaspoon salt*
½	*cup sour cream, liquid drained*
1	*tablespoon cider vinegar*
¼	*teaspoon dill*

Peel and thinly slice the cucumber and sprinkle the salt over the slices. Refrigerate the cucumber slices for 1 hour. Rinse them thoroughly with cold water to remove the salt. In a mixing bowl combine the sour cream, vinegar, and dill together. Toss the cucumbers with the sour cream dressing.

MAKES 4 TO 6 SERVINGS

Sweet & Sour Cucumber Salad

This is a regular member of the sweets and sours array on the salad bar. Slice the onions and the cucumbers see-through thin.

1	*red onion*	3	*cups water*
3	*medium cucumbers*	1	*teaspoon dried dill weed*
½	*cup sugar*	1	*teaspoon salt*
1	*cup cider vinegar*	¼	*teaspoon pepper*

Peel the onion and cucumbers and slice them very thinly. In a large mixing bowl mix the sugar, vinegar, water, dill, salt, and pepper. Pour this mixture over the cucumbers and onion. Let the mixture soak for 1 hour in the refrigerator. Serve cold.

MAKES 4 TO 6 SERVINGS

SEVEN SWEETS AND SEVEN SOURS

Appetite never had so stirring a team of cheerleaders as the seven sweets and seven sours of the Pennsylvania Dutch table. Colorful, brilliantly flavored, and singing of farm kitchens and a good harvest, this felicitous culinary tradition makes dinner in Dutch country a thrill ride for taste buds.

To fully understand the appeal of seven sweets and seven sours, it is essential to understand the meaning of dinner. As a noontime meal coming at the end of a long morning's work in the fields, dinner in Pennsylvania Dutch country is a foursquare feast of hearty fare for people who burn calories by the tens of thousands. Ham or fresh pork, whole roasted turkey or pot pies thick with dumplings, and roast beef or meat loaf are surrounded by constellations of such stalwart side dishes as mashed potatoes, bread filling, steamed cabbage, corn pudding, onion pie, and Dutch turnips. And there will be bread, too—cornbread, white bread, dinner rolls—and of course pies and cakes for dessert.

Seven sweets and seven sours are never the stars of a meal—that's a role for the roast or a casserole—but they are a supporting cast with brio. The name may not literally be correct, for it is not uncommon to find meals at which there are far more than merely seven bowls of sweet and/or tangy preserved vegetables and fruits on the table. However many there are, they are characterized by variety and bright, brilliant flavors—exactly the rejuvenation a palate needs in the midst of a meal defined by monumental heaps of protein and starch. Seven sweets and seven sours are zesty and pickly, teasing the tongue back into action for second helpings of ham and cabbage stew.

They are also a shining example of the skill of the farm kitchen. Canning, spicing, pickling, and curing are still alive and well in Pennsylvania Dutch country, where these talents originally served housewives who had no ready access to grocery stores and for whom

even the yield of a seasonal garden could not be relied on to supply what was needed at any given time of year. To survive and to eat well, a homemaker had to know how to put up tomatoes, corn, and other fruits and vegetables when they were abundant so they could be put on the table out of season.

Dinner was the opportunity for a cook to show off her preserving skills. History is unclear as to whether there was ever a custom of putting exactly seven sweet things and seven sour things on the table or whether that term simply became a way of expressing the bounty of the pickled spread. Some accounts say that the ritual became so much a part of Pennsylvania Dutch hospitality that guests would count what was on the table and merrily reprimand a hostess whose total didn't add up to fourteen, exactly half and half.

Nowadays, few guests are sticklers for precise numbers, but regulars who come for dinner at the Dutch Kitchen know they can count on well over a dozen sweets and sours on the salad bar. Among the essentials are pepper cabbage, chow-chow, five-cup salad, red beet pickled eggs, sweet and sour cucumbers, and creamy cucumbers.

If these kinds of pickled things are your idea of edible bliss, you should know about Kitchen Kettle Village in the town of Intercourse in the heart of Pennsylvania Dutch country. Every third weekend in September, Kitchen Kettle Village hosts a Seven Sweets and Seven Sours Festival. Begun a quarter century ago simply as a way to celebrate the harvest, it has become an opportunity for cooks to show off their skills at making local vegetables into condiments and relishes. Opportunities abound to taste not only traditional chow-chows, red beet eggs, and three-bean salads but also such exotica as four-berry jelly, hot pepper jam, pickled portobellos, and peanut butter schmier.

Pickled Eggs

A favorite pucker-upper throughout eastern Pennsylvania, as well as in old-time taverns around the nation, pickled eggs are one of the most colorful players on the Dutch Kitchen salad bar.

1	cup white vinegar
3	cups red beet juice
	Several sliced red beets
12	cloves
½	teaspoon salt
½	teaspoon black pepper
2	cloves garlic, coarsely chopped
12	hard-cooked eggs

In a medium saucepan combine the vinegar, beet juice, beets, cloves, salt, pepper, and garlic and bring to a slow boil. Stir for about 2 minutes. Place the hard-cooked eggs in a glass fruit jar and slowly pour the boiling vinegar mixture over them. Cover and refrigerate for several days. The longer the eggs stay in the vinegar, the stronger they become.

MAKES 1 DOZEN

Three-Bean Salad

This is a dish that can be found on the salad bar or purchased from hutches of jellies, salads, and relishes. It is an easy one to make for any picnic.

1	medium onion
1	(24-ounce) can green beans, drained
1	(24-ounce) can wax beans, drained
1	(24-ounce) can kidney beans, drained
1	cup sugar
1	cup white vinegar
2	cups water

Peel and slice the onion. In a large mixing bowl combine the onion, green beans, wax beans, and kidney beans. In a separate mixing bowl combine the sugar, vinegar, and water. Pour this mixture over the bean mixture. Let soak in the refrigerator and serve cold.

MAKES 18 SERVINGS

Potato Salad

Potato salad recipes are like snowflakes: No two are exactly alike. But one thing that distinguishes almost all the potato salads served in Pennsylvania Dutch country is that they contain plenty of eggs.

8	medium potatoes
4	hard-cooked eggs, chopped
1	small onion, chopped
1	cup chopped celery
1½	teaspoons salt
2	cups mayonnaise
¼	cup white vinegar
¼	teaspoon celery seed
1	teaspoon Dijon mustard

Peel the potatoes and cut them into quarters. Place the potatoes in a large stockpot of water and boil until they are cooked through. Drain and rinse the potatoes with cold water. Let them cool. In a large mixing bowl comine the eggs, onion, celery, salt, mayonnaise, vinegar, celery seed, and Dijon mustard. Mix well. Fold in the potatoes to coat with the dressing.

MAKES 8 TO 10 SERVINGS

Hot Potato Salad

Ahhh, hot potato salad. What a delectable balance of sweet sugar, savory bacon, and tart vinegar. It's the perfect flavor in which to bathe soft nuggets of warm potato.

6	slices bacon
½	cup chopped celery
1	small onion, chopped
1	tablespoon all-purpose flour
1½	teaspoons salt
⅓	cup sugar
⅓	cup white vinegar
⅔	cup water
4	cups hot cooked potatoes, diced
¼	teaspoon pepper
1	tablespoon chopped fresh parsley

Cut the bacon into small pieces and fry in a skillet until crisp. Remove the bacon and drain, reserving 2 tablespoons of drippings. Sauté the celery and onion in the drippings. Add the flour to blend. Add the salt, sugar, vinegar, and water. Bring to a boil, stirring constantly. Pour this dressing over the potatoes in a large bowl. Crumble the bacon slices on top. Sprinkle with pepper and parsley and serve warm.

MAKES 8 SERVINGS

Red Beet Salad

Arrays of sweets and sours always contain beets in different forms, sometimes for their color (as in red beet pickled eggs), but also for their earthy sweetness.

3	cups sliced red beets
1	small onion, sliced
1	cup red beet juice
½	cup sugar
2	cups white vinegar

In a medium mixing bowl, combine the beets and onion. Add the beet juice, sugar, and vinegar. Mix gently. Let the mixture sit in the refrigerator for 1 hour. Serve chilled.

MAKES 6 SERVINGS

Applesauce Salad

A special item on the salad bar, this "salad" of applesauce is embellished with dried fruit, shredded coconut, and walnuts. It's delicious . . . and healthful, too.

4	cups chunky applesauce
2	cups shredded coconut
2	cups raisins
1	cup chopped walnuts

In a medium mixing bowl combine the applesauce, coconut, raisins, and walnuts. Cover the bowl and refrigerate for 1 hour. Serve chilled.

MAKES 9 CUPS

· SOUPS ·

Maryland-Style Crab Soup

Crab Bisque

Mushroom Bisque

Turkey Noodle Soup

Turkey Corn Noodle Soup

Hearty Ham & Bean Soup

US Senate Ham
& Bean Soup

Chicken & Ham Gumbo

Captain's Ground Beef
& Vegetable Soup

Hamburger Soup

Beef, Barley
& Mushroom Soup

Hearty Beef Stew

Italian Wedding Soup

Italian Bean & Pasta Soup

Italian Sausage Stew

Cheese Tortellini Soup with White
Beans & Kielbasa

French Onion Soup

Cream of Potato Soup

Vegetarian Vegetable Soup

Manhattan-Style Clam Chowder

New England-Style Clam Chowder

Corn Chowder

Mariners Garden Chowder

Chicken Corn Chowder

Cabbage Soup

Bavarian Cabbage

Split Pea Soup

Lentil Soup

Pumpkin Soup
with Honey & Cloves

Maryland-Style Crab Soup

Tom is the soup master at the Dutch Kitchen, and this is one of his very favorites. He especially likes to make it in the late summer when the corn is fresh and taken straight off the cob.

3	tablespoons vegetable oil
1	small onion, chopped
2	cups chopped celery
2	cups chopped carrots
12	cups clam stock
1	(16-ounce) can crushed tomatoes
1	(16-ounce) can tomato juice
1	cup corn, off the cob
1	teaspoon Old Bay seasoning
½	teaspoon celery seed
¼	teaspoon red pepper
	Black pepper
1	pound shredded crabmeat
2	cups cubed potatoes

Heat the oil in a large stockpot and sauté the onion, celery, and carrots. Add the clam stock, crushed tomatoes, tomato juice, clam juice, corn, Old Bay, celery seed, red pepper, black pepper to taste, and crab. Allow the soup to simmer for 30 minutes. Add the potatoes and continue simmering until the potatoes are tender. Remove the soup from the heat and serve.

MAKES 14 TO 16 SERVINGS

Crab Bisque

This may be our most popular and most requested soup recipe," Tom says. "I had to ask myself, 'Do we really want to give out this recipe?' Then I thought what a shame it would be if it could not go on and be remembered for generations."

1	tablespoon butter
1	cup minced onion
2	cups minced celery
4	cups shredded crabmeat
1	tablespoon all-purpose flour
12	cups chicken stock
1	(16-ounce) can clam juice
1	bay leaf
1	teaspoon Old Bay seasoning
	Salt and pepper
4	cups half-and-half

Heat the butter in a stockpot over medium heat. Sauté the onion, celery, crab, and flour. Add the chicken stock, clam juice, bay leaf, Old Bay, and salt and pepper to taste. Let the soup simmer for 10 to 15 minutes. Add the half-and-half and remove from the heat. Discard the bay leaf and serve.

MAKES 8 TO 10 SERVINGS

Mushroom Bisque

Dr. Frank Palermo and his wife, Betty, are nearly everyday regulars at the Dutch Kitchen. Their table is always ready. If they are planning not to come in for lunch one day, they will call the restaurant and let the staff know that the table can be given to someone else. Betty enjoys this bisque so much that Tom once traded his recipe for it in order to get her recipe for fudge. He describes that as a win-win situation.

2	*pounds fresh mushrooms*
8	*cups chicken broth*
2	*medium onions, chopped*
½	*teaspoon white pepper*
½	*teaspoon Tabasco sauce*
¾	*cup (1 ½ sticks) butter*
¾	*cup all-purpose flour*
8	*cups half-and-half*
¼	*cup sherry (optional)*

Chop the mushrooms and stems very finely by hand or with a food processor. In a stockpot over medium heat, simmer the mushrooms, chicken broth, onions, white pepper, and Tabasco for 30 minutes. Meanwhile, prepare a roux to be used just before serving. Melt the butter in a saucepan. Add the flour and whisk until well blended. Add the half-and-half to the simmering mushroom soup. Turn up the heat and, while stirring, bring the soup almost to boiling. Stir in the roux to achieve the desired consistency for serving.

MAKES 8 TO 10 SERVINGS

Turkey Noodle Soup

Why turkey and not chicken? Tom explains, "Turkey meat will not break down or become stringy as does chicken when it sits in soup urns for an extended period of time."

1	cup diced onion
1	cup diced carrots
2	cups diced celery
3	tablespoons vegetable oil
1	teaspoon dried thyme
¼	teaspoon black pepper
1	teaspoon salt
12	cups chicken or turkey stock
3	cups cooked turkey, chopped into bite-size pieces
2	cups egg noodles
1	teaspoon chopped fresh parsley

In a large stockpot sauté the onion, carrots, and celery in the oil. Add the thyme, pepper, and salt. Add the chicken or turkey stock. Bring the soup to a boil for about 25 minutes. Add the turkey, noodles, and parsley. Once the noodles reach the right tenderness, remove the soup from the heat and serve.

MAKES 8 TO 10 SERVINGS

Variations: Add cooked white rice in place of egg noodles for chicken or turkey rice soup.

Turkey Corn Noodle Soup

When Tom was a boy and went out to dinner with his parents, this was the soup he liked to order most. "It was simple," he recalls. "Chicken or turkey, corn, and noodles—the ingredients most kids like."

1	cup diced onion
1	cup diced carrots
2	cups diced celery
1½	cups whole corn (taken from the cob or frozen)
3	tablespoons vegetable oil
½	teaspoon dried thyme
¼	teaspoon black pepper
1	teaspoon salt
3	quarts chicken or turkey stock
3	cups cooked turkey, chopped into bite-size pieces
2	cups egg noodles
1	teaspoon chopped fresh parsley

In a large stockpot sauté the onion, carrots, celery, and corn in the oil for 20 minutes. Add the thyme, pepper, and salt. Add the chicken or turkey stock. Bring the soup to a boil and continue boiling for 25 minutes. Add the turkey, noodles, and parsley. Once the noodles reach the right tenderness, remove from the heat and serve.

MAKES 8 TO 10 SERVINGS

Hearty Ham & Bean Soup

Tom makes ham and bean soup just the way his mother taught him. He believes it is equally as satisfying at a summer holiday picnic as on a cool rainy day.

2	cups dried assorted beans and peas (navy, split pea, lima, lentil, black- eyed)
8	cups water
1	meaty smoked ham hock
1	cup diced celery
½	cup diced carrot
¼	cup diced onion
2	cups diced potatoes
1	cup diced tomato
1	bay leaf
½	teaspoon black pepper
1	teaspoon dried thyme
1	teaspoon dried parsley

Place the assorted beans in a container. Cover with water two inches over the beans and soak for 8 to 10 hours or overnight. Drain the beans and place them in a large soup pot with the 8 cups water. Add the ham hock and boil until the meat becomes tender, about 35 minutes. When the meat is tender, remove the hock and pick the ham from the bone. Continue simmering the beans in the pot. Discard the hock and cut the ham into bite-size pieces. Return the ham to the pot. When the beans are just about tender, about 1 hour, add the celery, carrot, onion, potatoes, tomato, bay leaf, pepper, thyme, and parsley. Simmer until the beans are ready and the potatoes are tender. It will take about 20 minutes. Remove from the heat, discard the bay leaf, and serve.

MAKES 6 TO 8 SERVINGS

U.S. Senate Ham & Bean Soup

When told that my Hearty Ham & Bean Soup should not have carrot or tomato in it, I was insulted," Tom says. "That's the only way to make it, and the only way that I ever had it. However, I did discover U.S. Senate Ham & Bean soup, which is virtually white and without the tomatoes and carrots. Now our customers—and I—enjoy both variations equally."

2	cups dried great Northern beans
1	meaty smoked ham hock
8	cups water
1	cup diced celery
¼	cup diced onion
2	medium potatoes, minced, or 1½ cups leftover mashed potatoes
1	teaspoon black pepper
1	teaspoon dried thyme
1	teaspoon dried parsley

Place the beans in a container. Cover with water two inches over the beans and soak for 8 to 10 hours or overnight. Drain the beans and place them in a large soup pot with the water. Add the ham hock and boil until the meat becomes tender. When the meat is tender, remove the hock and pick the ham from the bone. Continue simmering the beans in the pot. Discard the hock and cut the ham into bite-size pieces. Return the ham to the pot. When the beans are just about tender (1 to 1 ½ hours) add the celery, onion, potatoes, pepper, thyme, and parsley. Simmer until the beans are ready. Remove from the heat and serve.

MAKES 6 TO 8 SERVINGS

Chicken & Ham Gumbo

You'll find this festive dish on the menu in the spring around Mardi Gras time. It's a nice precursor to the Lenten season.

2	cups diced onions
1	tablespoon diced garlic
½	head red cabbage, shredded
1	cup olive oil
¼	cup all-purpose flour
2	cups chopped cooked chicken
16	cups chicken broth
1	cup diced tomato
2	bay leaves
1	teaspoon dried thyme
	Salt and pepper
½	teaspoon crushed red pepper
2	cups cooked rice
1	cup chopped cooked ham
2	cups okra, fresh or frozen

In a large stockpot sauté the onions, garlic, and cabbage in olive oil. Stir in the flour and chicken. Add the chicken broth, tomato, bay leaves, thyme, salt and pepper to taste, red pepper, rice, and ham. Let the soup simmer for 30 minutes. Add the okra and cook about 10 minutes longer. Discard the bay leaves and serve.

MAKES 14 TO 16 SERVINGS

Captain's Ground Beef & Vegetable Soup

Joyce Gallagher, a fifteen-plus-year member of the staff, used to sing the praises of a soup once served at a restaurant called the Corner House, where she was a waitress. Joyce explained to cook Billy Rumble what was in it and how to make it; and it has since become part of the Dutch Kitchen repertoire.

1	pound ground beef
¼	cup olive oil
2	medium onions, diced
1	rib celery, chopped
1	cup diced green pepper
1	(16-ounce) can V8 vegetable juice
1	(16-ounce) bag frozen mixed vegetables
1	(10¾-ounce) can cream of mushroom soup
1	(10¾-ounce) can cream of celery soup

Brown the ground beef. In a large stockpot heat the oil over medium heat and sauté the onion, celery, and green pepper. Add the V8 juice, mixed vegetables, soups, and ground beef. Cover and simmer the soup until the vegetables are tender. Remove from the heat and serve.

MAKES 12 SERVINGS

Hamburger Soup

An old-time favorite, Hamburger Soup, has been on the Dutch Kitchen menu since the early days. This warm, filling soup is especially welcome on a cold day.

1½   *pounds ground beef, browned*

2   *medium potatoes, cubed*

2   *tablespoons olive oil*

1   *onion, diced*

1   *rib celery, diced*

3   *cups crushed tomatoes*

      Salt and pepper

8   *cups beef stock*

1   *cup elbow macaroni*

4   *hard-cooked eggs, diced*

Brown the ground beef, in a skillet and drain; set aside. In a separate pot cook the potatoes in boiling water until tender, about 10 minutes. Heat the olive oil in a stockpot over medium heat and sauté the onions and celery. Add the browned beef, tomatoes, beef stock, and salt and pepper to taste. Add the macaroni noodles and let soup simmer until the noodles are tender. Immediately before removing the soup from the heat, stir in the eggs and potatoes.

MAKES 8 TO 10 SERVINGS

Beef, Barley & Mushroom Soup

This is a great rainy-day soup. Barley and mushrooms are common groceries in a well-stocked Pennsylvania Dutch kitchen.

¾   *cup uncooked medium barley*

2   *tablespoons vegetable oil*

1   *cup chopped onion*

2   *cups chopped carrots*

2   *cups chopped celery*

12   *cups beef stock*

1   *pound mushrooms, sliced*

¼   *teaspoon black pepper*

Cook the barley according to package directions. Heat the oil in a large stockpot over medium heat. Sauté the onion, carrots, and celery. Add the beef stock, mushrooms, and pepper. Let the soup simmer for 20 to 30 minutes before adding the cooked barley. When the soup is hot, remove it from the heat and serve.

MAKES 14 TO 16 SERVINGS

Hearty Beef Stew

Looking for comfort from cold weather? Look no further than this classic beef stew recipe, which is a deeply satisfying one-dish meal—with a quick trip through the salad bar to begin, of course.

3	tablespoons oil
1½	pounds beef cubes
1	teaspoon salt
½	teaspoon black pepper
5	cups beef stock
1	medium onion, diced
1	cup chopped celery
1	cup chopped carrots
2	cups tomato juice
1	cup diced tomato
¼	teaspoon dried rosemary
¼	teaspoon dried marjoram
½	teaspoon dried thyme
3	potatoes, peeled and quartered
4	tablespoons butter
4	tablespoons all-purpose flour

Heat the oil in a large stockpot over medium-high heat. Saute the beef cubes and season with the salt and pepper. Add the beef stock, onion, celery, and carrots and simmer for 45 minutes. Add the tomato juice, tomato, rosemary, marjoram, and thyme. Bring to a boil and add the potatoes. Once the potatoes are tender, remove the stew from the heat. In a small saucepan melt the butter and whisk in the flour until well blended. Add the roux to the stew to thicken if desired. Turn down the heat and let the stew simmer on low for 1 hour. Serve hot.

MAKES 4 TO 6 SERVINGS

Italian Wedding Soup

Found in restaurants throughout the heartland, Italian Wedding Soup is more Italian-American than it is Italian. Apparently its name comes not from the fact that it once was very popular at Italian weddings in the USA (which it was), but because the combination of meat and greens makes such a good couple, culinarily speaking. Thank you, Deb, for bringing it back.

MEATBALLS:

12	ounces ground beef
½	cup breadcrumbs
1	egg, well beaten
1	small onion, finely minced
1	tablespoon chopped fresh parsley
½	teaspoon salt
½	garlic clove, chopped
1	tablespoon grated Parmesan cheese
¼	teaspoon dried oregano

SOUP STOCK:

2	tablespoons olive oil
1	small onion, diced
2	cups diced carrots
2	cups diced celery
16	cups chicken stock
1	cup chopped kale or endive
1	tablespoon grated Parmesan cheese
1	hard-cooked egg, chopped
1	cup acini di pepe noodles

Preheat the oven to 350°F.

For the meatballs, combine the ground beef, breadcrumbs, egg, onion, parsley, salt, garlic, Parmesan cheese, and oregano in a large mixing bowl; mix well. Be careful not to overmix since it could toughen the beef. Form small meatballs to ¾-inch in diameter, lay them on a baking sheet, and place them in the oven for 20 minutes, or until well cooked.

To prepare the soup stock, heat the olive oil in a large stockpot over medium heat. Sauté the onion, carrots, and celery. Add the chicken stock and bring to a boil. Add the meatballs, kale, Parmesan cheese, egg, and noodles. Remove from the heat to serve.

MAKES 8 TO 10 SERVINGS

Italian Bean & Pasta Soup

I don't know where, when, or how this recipe started," Tom says. "It's prepared and served at the restaurant every month and it works. And like they say, "If it works, don't fix it."

1	cup chopped onion
3	tablespoons olive oil
2	cups chopped celery
1	cup chopped carrots
2	garlic cloves, minced
1	teaspoon salt
½	teaspoon pepper
1	(16-ounce) can crushed tomatoes
6	cups chicken stock
1	teaspoon dried basil
1	teaspoon dried thyme
1	(8-ounce) can kidney beans
1	cup cooked elbow macaroni

In a large stockpot sauté the onion in the oil until they are tender. Add the celery, carrots, garlic, salt, and pepper. Cook the vegetables for 5 minutes. Add the tomatoes, chicken stock, basil, and thyme. Bring to a boil. Add the kidney beans and simmer for a few minutes. Add the noodles and simmer until they are tender. Remove from the heat and serve.

MAKES 4 TO 6 SERVINGS

Italian Sausage Stew

The full, satisfying flavor of this soup is based on the combination of sweet sausage and coarsely chopped vegetables.

2	tablespoons olive oil
1	cup chopped onion
2	cups chopped celery
1	cup chopped carrot
1	cup chopped green bell pepper
½	tablespoon minced garlic
½	teaspoon dried basil
½	teaspoon dried oregano
½	teaspoon dried thyme
12	cups beef stock
1	(16-ounce) can diced tomatoes
1	pound sweet Italian sausage, cooked
2	medium potatoes, cubed

In a stockpot heat the oil over medium heat. Sauté the onion, celery, carrot, green pepper, and garlic. Stir in the basil, oregano, and thyme. Add the beef stock, tomatoes, and Italian sausage. Bring the soup to a boil and cook for 15 minutes. Add the potatoes and simmer until they are tender, about 10 minutes. Remove from the heat and serve.

MAKES 8 TO 10 SERVINGS

Cheese Tortellini Soup with White Beans & Kielbasa

Good kielbasa is a hallmark of Schuylkill County in general and the dinner tables of Frackville in particular. Of all the dishes in which it's used at the restaurant, this is one of our personal favorites: a multi-ethnic soup that expresses the anything-goes nature of the American melting pot.

1	pound smoked kielbasa
¼	cup olive oil
1	cup chopped onion
1	whole fennel bulb, chopped
½	teaspoon minced garlic
1	teaspoon dried thyme
½	teaspoon crushed red pepper
12	cups chicken stock
1	pound chopped kale
1	(8-ounce) can white kidney beans, washed and drained
1	pound frozen cheese tortellini
	Freshly grated Parmesan cheese

In a covered stockpot boil the kielbasa for 25 minutes. Let it cool before slicing into ¼-inch thick pieces. In a large stockpot, heat the olive oil and sauté the onion, fennel, and garlic. Add the thyme and crushed red pepper. Add the chicken stock, kale, and kidney beans. Let the soup simmer. Just before serving add the tortellini and bring to a boil. Sprinkle each serving with fresh Parmesan cheese.

MAKES 14 TO 16 SERVINGS

From the German word sechs, *meaning six, the* hex signs originally had six-pointed stars. These signs are welcoming symbols of faith, good luck, happiness, and love.

Frackville's Flag Street exposes the quaint mining town's patriotism.

The diner has come a long way since it first moved to Frackville in 1971.

True to its roots the Famous Dutch Kitchen Restaurant has kept the diner feel with flipcard jukeboxes and original stools and counter.

Famous of Pennsylvania Dutch cooking are the 7 sweets and 7 sours (pages 55–57) found in the fantastic salad bar.

Cheese Tortellini Soup with White Beans & Kielbasa
(page 80)

Dutch Kitchen's famous
fresh baked cornbread
(page 24)

Turkey and mixed vegetables served over a fresh baked waffle (page 16, see variation)

Pineapple Glazed Smoked Ham Steak (page 170)

Start your day with a grilled sticky bun (page 14).

Get vertical with an Atomic Banana Split (page 98).

Shoo Fly Cake
(page 182)

Banana Cake
(page 187)
layered with sliced
banana and topped
with Creamy
Peanut Butter Icing
(page 189)

French Onion Soup

Joyce Hereshko, a Dutch Kitchen waitress since 1973, was asked peoples' reaction over the years to the Kitchen's French onion soup. While not normally a person of few words, she didn't need many to answer: "They love it."

½   *cup (1 stick) butter*

4   *cups chopped onions*

8   *cups beef stock*

2   *tablespoons Parmesan cheese*

     Salt and pepper

2   *cups croutons*

     Shredded mozzarella cheese

In a stockpot heat the butter over medium heat. Sauté the onions until tender. Add the beef stock, Parmesan cheese, and salt and pepper to taste. Let the soup simmer for 25 minutes. Top each serving with some croutons and mozzarella cheese as desired.

MAKES 6 TO 8 SERVINGS

Cream of Potato Soup

There is much debate among the staff of the Dutch Kitchen about exactly how the potato soup should be made. This recipe is the one used by Michelle Morgan, and most of the other potato-soup cooks are willing to admit it is the best.

½	plus ¼ cup butter
1	cup diced onion
2	cups diced celery
¼	cup diced carrot
1	teaspoon white pepper
10	cups chicken stock
2	cups half-and-half
6	medium potatoes, cubed
1	hard-cooked egg, chopped
½	cup all-purpose flour
	Chopped fresh chives

Heat ¼ cup of the butter in a stockpot and sauté the onion, celery, carrot, and white pepper. Add the chicken stock and bring to a boil. Lower the heat. Stir in the half-and-half, potatoes, and egg. Let the soup simmer until the potatoes are tender. Prepare a roux by melting the remaining ½ cup butter in a small saucepan and stirring in the flour. Mix well and then add the roux slowly to the soup until the desired consistency is reached. Top with the chives to serve.

MAKES 8 TO 10 SERVINGS

Vegetarian Vegetable Soup

As substantial as any meat-based soup, this one gets it oomph from plenty of potatoes, carrots, and onion.

1	cup cubed potato
3	tablespoons olive oil
1	cup diced onion
2	cups chopped celery
½	teaspoon garlic powder
½	teaspoon dried thyme
1	bay leaf
	Salt and pepper
1	(16-ounce) can vegetable juice
1	(16-ounce) can crushed tomatoes
1	(16-ounce) bag frozen mixed vegetables
4	cups water

In a large stockpot heat the oil over medium heat and sauté the onion, celery, garlic powder, thyme, bay leaf, and salt and pepper to taste. Add the V8 juice, crushed tomatoes, mixed vegetables, and water. Bring the soup to a boil. Reduce the heat and simmer for 10 minutes. Add the potatoes and simmer until they are tender, about 20 minutes. Remove the soup from the heat, discard the bay leaf, and serve.

MAKES 8 TO 10 SERVINGS

Manhattan-Style Clam Chowder

For as long as one can remember, the Dutch Kitchen has rotated Manhattan and New England-style clam chowders on Fridays. The locals already know that. Now you do, too. It's something you can count on every week; and if you have a favorite, plan your visit around which one is being served.

3	strips bacon
1	cup chopped onion
1	cup chopped celery
1	(16-ounce) bag frozen chopped clams
1	teaspoon dried thyme
1	teaspoon black pepper
1	teaspoon Old Bay seasoning
1	(16-ounce) can clam juice
2	cups chopped carrots
1	(16-ounce) can crushed tomatoes
8	cups water
2	tablespoons clam base
1	(16-ounce) can tomato juice
2	cups cubed potatoes

In a large stockpot fry the bacon until it's crisp. Remove the bacon, chop it, and return it to the stockpot. Sauté, in the bacon drippings, the chopped bacon, onion, celery, clams, thyme, black pepper, Old Bay, clam juice, carrots, and crushed tomatoes. Add the water, clam base, and tomato juice. Bring the soup to a boil and add the potatoes. Once the potatoes are tender, remove the soup from the heat and serve.

MAKES 12 TO 14 SERVINGS

New England-Style Clam Chowder

Tom says, "Just because Frackville is located far from the seacoast doesn't mean we don't appreciate a good New England chowder." In fact, soups made from clams, crabs, or oysters have always been an important part of the eastern Pennsylvania diet.

3	strips bacon
1	cup chopped onion
1	cup chopped celery
1	(16-ounce) bag frozen chopped clams
1	teaspoon dried thyme
1	teaspoon black pepper
1	(16-ounce) can clam juice
4	cups water
2	tablespoons clam base
4	cups half-and-half
2	cups cubed potatoes
¼	cup (½ stick) butter
¼	cup all-purpose flour

In a large stockpot fry the bacon until it's crisp. Remove the bacon, chop it, and return it to the stockpot. Sauté, in the bacon drippings, the chopped bacon, onion, celery, clams, thyme, black pepper, and clam juice. Add the water and bring the soup to a boil. Add the clam base and half-and-half and simmer. Add the potatoes and continue to simmer the soup while preparing the roux. In a separate pan melt the butter and whisk in the flour until smooth. Once the potatoes are tender, remove the soup from the heat and stir in the roux until the right consistency is achieved for serving.

MAKES 12 TO 14 SERVINGS

Note: We generate a lot of bacon fat in the restaurant. Here's an idea taken from the Patio Room at Hess's: Reserve the bacon fat and use it to prepare your roux instead of using butter. It will add great flavor. Thanks, Cary.

Corn Chowder

Farmhouse chowder is a Lancaster County tradition. It's a substantial meal made from cupboard staples.

8	strips bacon
1	large onion, chopped
2	tablespoons all-purpose flour
4	cups chicken stock
5	cups dried corn
4	cups half-and-half
3	potatoes, cubed

Cut the strips of bacon into ¼-inch pieces. Fry the bacon and remove from the frying pan. Sauté the onion in the remaining bacon fat. Add the flour and bacon pieces to the onion and mix well. Add the chicken stock and corn. Bring to a boil and simmer for 20 minutes. Add the half-and-half and potatoes. Let the chowder simmer until the potatoes are tender, about 10 minutes. Serve hot.

MAKES 6 TO 8 SERVINGS

Mariners Garden Chowder

You will be able to dip your spoon into this soup on Friday or Sunday at the Dutch Kitchen. It has a rich base, and its character can be changed by adding different kinds of seafood. As Tom puts it, "This soup has no rules."

2	tablespoons olive oil
1	cup diced onion
1	cup diced carrots
1	cup diced celery
1	(16-ounce) can tomato juice
1	(16-ounce) can diced tomatoes
4	cups chicken stock
½	cup baby shrimp
1	cup chopped haddock or scrod
1	cup chopped clam pieces
1	cup cooked rice

Heat the oil in a stockpot over medium heat and sauté the onion, carrots, and celery. Add the tomato juice and diced tomatoes and cook, stirring, for 5 minutes. Add the chicken stock and simmer for 15 minutes. Add the shrimp, haddock, and clam pieces. Cover and let the soup simmer for 15 more minutes. Add the rice just before serving.

MAKES 8 TO 10 SERVINGS

Chicken Corn Chowder

This Lancaster County staple is a cream soup with a chicken base enriched with the heartiness of corn and potatoes. It is a special favorite of long-time waitress Diane, who is known for asking elderly gents dining with their wives, "When are you going to get rid of her so we can start spending time together?" Tom describes Diane as "brash, funny, and confident . . . always comes out smelling like a rose."

½	plus 1 sticks butter
2	small onions, diced
3	to 4 celery ribs, diced
8	cups chicken broth
2	cups diced cooked chicken
1	(10-ounce) package frozen corn, thawed
3	cups cubed potatoes
2	cups half-and-half
½	cup all-purpose flour
1	hard-cooked egg, chopped

Heat ½ stick of the butter in a skillet over medium-high heat. Sauté the onions until soft. Add the diced celery, chicken broth, chicken, corn, and potatoes. Cover, bring to a boil, and simmer for 10 minutes. Once the potatoes are tender, add the half-and-half. Heat, but do not bring to a boil. Prepare a roux to be used just before serving by melting the remaining 1 stick of butter in a saucepan over medium-high heat and adding the flour. Stir or whisk until well blended and set aside. When the soup is heated and ready to be removed for serving, stir in the roux to gain the right consistency. It should be smooth, but not too thick. Sprinkle the chopped egg onto the soup just before serving.

MAKES 8 TO 10 SERVINGS

Cabbage Soup

Tony Antz and his son Chris, are in charge of the heavy maintenance at the Dutch Kitchen. "We know how clean this place is," Chris declared one afternoon as he and his men gathered around a large table in the dining room for a meal. This is one of their favorite soups. "It's their tough criticism that keeps us on our toes," Tom declares.

1	medium head cabbage, chopped
1	medium onion, chopped
¼	plus ¼ cup butter (1 stick)
4	cups chicken stock
1	teaspoon black pepper
2	cups half-and-half
¼	cup all-purpose flour

Sauté the cabbage and onion in a stockpot in ¼ cup of the butter. Add the chicken stock and black pepper and boil until the cabbage is tender, about 30 minutes. Reduce the heat, add the half-and-half, and allow the soup to simmer while preparing the roux. In a saucepan melt the remaining ¼ cup butter and whisk in the flour until smooth. Slowly add the roux to the soup and stir until desired consistency is reached. Serve immediately.

MAKES 3 TO 4 SERVINGS

Bavarian Cabbage

Tom created his own variation of a soup made long ago at the restaurant. He points out that, like so many other Pennsylvania Dutch recipes, each cook has his or her own way with it; and in his words, "My variation is undisputedly the best and will always receive a nod of approval from the best of the soup critics, my father-in-law, John Morgan."

1	meaty smoked ham hock
1	large head cabbage, chopped
12	cups water
1	(16-ounce) can diced tomatoes
1	(16-ounce) can tomato juice
1	teaspoon black pepper
3	medium potatoes, cubed

Boil the ham hock and cabbage in the water in a large stockpot. Once the cabbage begins to show tenderness, add the diced tomatoes and tomato juice and let simmer 15 minutes. Add the black pepper and potatoes. Once the potatoes are tender, remove from the heat and remove the ham hock. When the ham hock has cooled, remove the meat from the bone. Add the meat to the soup and serve.

MAKES 12 TO 14 SERVINGS

Split Pea Soup

Tom describes this as "a true Dutch Kitchen classic, usually prepared by Andrea Rockwell. Her touch of experience is evident by its great consistency. It satisfies not only our paying customers, but also her youngest critics—our own children, Thomas, Caroline, and Michael."

2	cups split peas
10	cups water
1	ham hock
½	cup chopped onion
1	cup chopped celery
½	cup chopped carrots
1	garlic clove, chopped
1	bay leaf
¼	teaspoon dried thyme
	Black pepper
2	potatoes, cubed

Cook the peas covered in the water with the ham hock for 1½ hours. Add the onion, celery, and carrots and cook for 30 minutes more. Add the garlic, bay leaf, thyme, and pepper to taste. Remove the ham hock. Shred the meat from the bone and add the meat to the soup along with the cubed potatoes. Once the potatoes are tender, remove the soup from the heat. Discard the bay leaf and serve.

MAKES 6 TO 8 SERVINGS

Lentil Soup

There is no vegetable more rib-sticking than the lentil, which is why so many vegetarian soups are based on it. This recipe augments its heartiness with cubed potatoes.

2	cups lentils
10	cups water
1	ham hock
½	cup chopped onion
1	cup chopped celery
¼	teaspoon thyme
	Black pepper
2	potatoes, cubed

Put the lentils in a stockpot and cover them with the water. Add the ham hock to the lentils and cook over low heat for 1½ hours. Add the onion and celery and cook the lentils for 30 minutes more. Season with the thyme and pepper to taste. Remove the ham hock. Shred the meat from the bone and add to the soup along with the potatoes. Once the potatoes are tender, remove the soup from the heat and serve.

MAKES 6 TO 8 SERVINGS

Pumpkin Soup with Honey & Cloves

For Tom Levkulic autumn in Pennsylvania means pumpkin soup. He advises anyone who makes it to use local honey. Not only will it taste "right," but it supports the local economy.

2	tablespoons butter
2	large carrots, finely diced
2	celery ribs, finely diced
1	large onion, finely diced
2	(15-ounce) cans pumpkin
6	cups chicken stock
¼	teaspoon cloves
¼	teaspoon cardamom
½	cup whipping cream
2	tablespoons honey

Melt the butter in a large soup pot on medium heat. Sauté the carrots, celery, and onion until tender. Purée the sautéed vegetables in a blender. Return the puréed vegetables to the soup pot. Add the pumpkin, chicken stock, cloves, and cardamom. Cover and simmer until heated through. Stir in the cream and honey and heat gently until the desired temperature. Serve immediately.

MAKES 6 TO 8 SERVINGS

PENNSYLVANIA DUTCH

Birds, hearts, and tulips are signs of welcome.

In a nation with so many impressive regional and ethnic meals, there is no table more awesome than one set for dinner in Pennsylvania Dutch country. The "Dutch" of southeastern Pennsylvania love to eat and to eat large. Their passion for food is such that they refer to themselves as *feinschmeckers*. An approximate translation is "people who eat well and plenty."

Even the casual linguist will note that *feinschmecker* sounds more German than Dutch. The people of this region are called—and call themselves—"Dutchmen." Their cooking is "Dutch," and it is not at all incongruous that the diner at exit 124 off I-81 is known as the Dutch Kitchen . . . despite the fact that it does not serve food from the

94

Netherlands. In fact, the Dutch of this region are of German descent and have little relationship to Holland.

The religious separatists who came to America from the Rhine Valley starting in the late seventeenth century called themselves *Pennsylvania Dutch* because it sounded like *Pennsylvania Deutch*, which is what they were. Their journey to the new world came after the Thirty Years War ravaged their homeland (and in fact earned the Union of Utrecht its independence from the German Empire). By the time the United States was founded, there were some 300,000 "Dutch" of various sects who were part of William Penn's Holy Experiment in religious tolerance. They included the Amish "Plain People" (who resolutely abjure modern technology) and more liberal settlers known as the "Gay Dutch."

The life of the Plain People endures unchanged, and their cultural legacy pervades the region. While they remain scrupulously plain, their antiquated ways have become a huge inspiration for all manner of

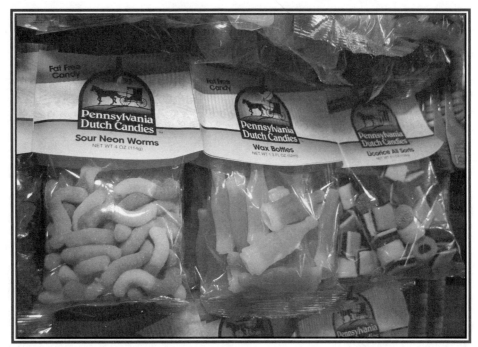

These candies on sale at the Dutch Kitchen, while not exactly Amish, exemplify the Pennsylvania Dutch love of sweets.

tourism, much of it—how shall we say?—of dubious taste. South of Frackville in the heart of Pennsylvania Dutch country, many of the restaurants serve meals of impressive quantity but questionable quality. These eating barns usually are part of a whole tourist-oriented complex where you can buy such tacky souvenirs as foot-long Amish novelty cigars and ridiculously big Amish sunglasses twice as wide as your head. Or there are the Amish wall plaques with epigrams such as "Nothin's More Beautiful Than a Woman Working." You can buy a book of Ferhoodled English with such amusing expressions and proverbs as "Aunt Minnie Sits Broad" (she's fat) and "A Plump Wife and a Big Barn Never Did Any Man Harm." Perhaps you need a gorilla-handed Amish back-scratcher, salt and pepper shakers of a black-suited man and woman with holes in their heads or a set of laminated plastic washable place mats with a picture of giggling barefoot Amish children peeking into an outhouse.

Enamel Speckleware is a country craft that dates back more than a century.

If you have never seen a real Amish person, it's enough to make you wonder: Are they really a race of garrulous bulimics who smoke jumbo cigars and leer at smutty jokes? No, the Amish themselves do not sell musical toilet paper dispensers, nor do they put their likenesses on highball glasses shaped like naked women's torsos. In the annals of exploitation for profit, few feats can compare to the way the Plain People have been adopted by energetic roadside entrepreneurs and turned into the quintessence of kitsch. The exquisite agony about the situation is that Amish people, although they shun their role as a tourist

attraction, are too humble and unworldly to complain.

Amish beliefs forbid compromise with contemporary manners. They drive horse-and-buggies instead of cars; they walk in high-top, button-hook shoes; and for entertainment they go to livestock auctions, not movies. They do not wear makeup or jewelry or even clothes with zippers, which they consider too modern. They look the same as they did centuries ago, before electricity and styling mousse for hair. To watch their daily comings and goings is to see the olden days, as you would in a museum of living folk life. But in this case, it's all for real.

Commercial bad taste notwithstanding, the heritage of the Pennsylvania Dutch people is profound. Their real crafts (as opposed to China-made mementoes) are exquisite and highly prized by collectors of folk art and rustic Americana, and their culinary heritage pervades the culture of the area far beyond their native Lancaster County. The Dutch Kitchen is a perfect example of how, in so many ways, Pennsylvania Dutch ways of eating have defined the cuisine of this region. You can see it in the very name of the restaurant, which founder John Morgan kept on the old diner when he moved it to Frackville simply because at the time he couldn't afford to put up another sign. The original owner, who established it down on I-78 on a highway many people took to visit Dutch land, christened it because he thought the word *Dutch* would appeal to travelers in search of local color.

Of greater importance than the name is the degree to which the Dutch Kitchen's menu reflects southeastern Pennsylvania's unique style of eating. "Them that work hard eat hearty," says the old Dutch proverb, and the kind of abundance due the hard-working farmer defines this restaurant's portions. The salad bar, with its echo of Seven Sweets and Seven Sours (see page 55), is spectacular all by itself. Meals of turkey or meat loaf come with *all* the fixins. Pies and cakes are sliced large. The Atomic Banana Split is the final solution to the most aggressive appetite.

An emphasis on soups, a wide variety of pork dishes (including scrapple for breakfast), and the abundant salad bar set the regional tone, but many of the menu's standbys are more specifically Pennsylvania Dutch. They include pot pies made with thick noodle dumplings, ham and cabbage casserole, smoked pork chops and local sausages, and rib-sticking bread filling (or stuffing) to go with roast turkey or meat loaf dinners. And for dessert, you can always count on shoo fly pie (and sometimes shoo fly cake) as well as big, simple—and simply wonderful—sugar cookies.

• SIDE DISHES •

Pennsylvania Dutch Chow-Chow

Baked Macaroni & Cheese

Baked Beans

Old-Fashioned Green Beans & Bacon

Baked Corn Supreme

Creamed Spinach

Stewed Tomatoes

Candied Sweet Potatoes

Mashed Potatoes

Scalloped Potatoes

Pennsylvania Dutch Filling
(Stuffing)

Blinis

Halushki

Parmesan Rice

Baked Apples

Shredded Lemon Pepper Cabbage

Pennsylvania Dutch Chow-Chow

Chow-chow is a relish of assorted pickled vegetables—whichever ones are on hand—that is always on the Dutch Kitchen salad bar. Tom suggests serving it as a salad or on the side of baked chicken or fish or to accompany Turkey Croquettes. He says, "The aroma of chow-chow on the stove is beyond compare."

2	cups cucumber, peeled and sliced
1	cup chopped green bell pepper
1	small head cabbage, chopped
2	cups green beans
1	cup lima beans
2	cups carrots
½	cup salt
8	plus 2 cups water
2	cups white vinegar
1	cup sugar
1	tablespoon turmeric
1	tablespoon mustard seed
1	tablespoon celery seed

In a large bowl combine the cucumber, green pepper, cabbage, green beans, lima beans, carrots, salt, and 8 cups of the water. Let soak overnight. Drain the vegetables. Pour the mixture into a large stockpot and cook over medium heat. Add the vinegar, sugar, turmeric, mustard seed, celery seed, and the remaining 2 cups water. Bring to a boil. Let cool and serve cold.

MAKES 6 SERVINGS

Baked Macaroni & Cheese

On our short list of supreme comfort foods that bring back the joys of nursery lunch, homemade macaroni and cheese, topped with a mantle of toasted breadcrumbs, is at the tippy top.

2	cups elbow macaroni
5	cups water
1	teaspoon salt
2	tablespoons butter
2	tablespoons all-purpose flour
1½	cups milk
1½	cups grated sharp Cheddar cheese
¼	cup plain breadcrumbs

Preheat the oven to 450°F. Put the macaroni in a saucepan. Add the water and salt, bring to a boil, and cook until tender; drain and set aside. Prepare a roux in a small saucepan on the stove or in the microwave by melting the butter and whisking in the flour, stirring to blend until thick and smooth. In a medium saucepan heat the milk almost to boiling. Add the cheese, stirring until melted. Slowly add the roux to the cheese mixture, stirring until smooth and well blended. Put the macaroni in a medium mixing bowl and pour the cheese sauce over the macaroni, stirring to blend. Spoon the macaroni into a greased 9 x 13-inch baking dish. Sprinkle with the breadcrumbs and bake for 30 minutes.

MAKES 6 SERVINGS

Baked Beans

 W e like to celebrate holidays at the Dutch Kitchen," Tom says. "What would be a typical picnic day for many is often celebrated here with family and friends." As Tom sees it, every patriotic holiday during the summer calls for baked beans.

1	pound navy beans
4	ounces bacon, chopped
1	small onion, chopped
1	teaspoon dry mustard
¼	cup brown sugar
2	teaspoons salt
¼	cup molasses
½	cup boiling water

Cover the beans with cold water and soak for 8 to 10 hours or overnight. When ready drain the beans. Put them in a large stockpot and cover them with water. Bring to a boil and cook for 30 minutes. Drain the beans and transfer them to an ovenproof pot. Add the bacon and onion. Preheat the oven to 250°F. In a bowl mix the dry mustard, sugar, salt, and molasses together and add to the beans. Add the water. Cover the pot and bake for about 6 hours, adding more water as necessary to cover the beans during baking. Remove the cover during the last hour of baking.

MAKES 8 SERVINGS

Old-Fashioned Green Beans & Bacon

Cook these beans until they are good and soft. An al dente snap texture goes against the luxurious nature of the dish.

12	*ounces green beans*
10	*slices bacon*
2	*medium potatoes, peeled and cubed*
1	*small onion, sliced*
¼	*cup water*
½	*teaspoon salt*

Cook the beans in a small amount of boiling, salted water in a saucepan for 10 to 15 minutes or until they are tender. Chop the bacon and fry it in a sauté pan over medium-high heat until crisp. Reduce the heat to medium. Combine the beans, potatoes, onion, water, and salt with the bacon and cook covered, about 15 minutes, or until the potatoes are tender.

MAKES 4 SERVINGS

Baked Corn Supreme

A luxurious casserole that can be served in tiny dabs as part of an appetizer platter or in larger portions to accompany meat and potatoes.

1	(15-ounce) can corn, drained
1½	teaspoons sugar
1	cup scalded milk
1	teaspoon salt
2	eggs, well beaten
1	tablespoon butter

Preheat the oven to 400°F. In a medium mixing bowl combine the corn, sugar, milk, salt, and eggs. Pour the mixture into a greased baking dish and bake for 40 minutes. Top with the butter.

MAKES 4 SERVINGS

Creamed Spinach

Creamed spinach goes especially well with red meat. It is an easy recipe, but don't make the mistake of only half-draining the spinach. Squeeze out all possible moisture before chopping it so you wind up with a thick, creamy texture.

1	pound fresh spinach
½	teaspoon salt
4	slices bacon, chopped
1	small onion, chopped
1	garlic clove, minced
2	tablespoons all-purpose flour
⅛	teaspoon black pepper
1	cup milk

Wash the spinach and remove the stems. Put the spinach in a steamer, add the salt, and steam the spinach until wilted. Drain the cooked spinach thoroughly, and chop it very finely. Cook the bacon, onion, and garlic in a heavy saucepan over medium heat until the onion is soft. Stir in the flour and pepper. Add the milk gradually, stirring constantly until boiling. Cook the sauce 2 minutes longer. Add the spinach to the sauce and mix well.

MAKES 4 SERVINGS

Stewed Tomatoes

The farm cook's repertoire is rich with recipes for tomatoes, which are on the table through the late summer . . . and well beyond, thanks to the traditions of canning and pickling and even making them into "summer mincemeat" for pie. Here is a recipe for stewed tomatoes that makes a good relish on the side for almost any meal.

1	cup chopped onion
½	cup olive oil
1	(16-ounce) can crushed tomatoes
½	cup sugar
1	tablespoon cornstarch
¼	cup warm water
1	(8-ounce) can diced tomatoes

In a skillet sauté the onion in the olive oil until they are tender. Stir in the crushed tomatoes and sugar. Blend together the cornstarch and water. Add to the skillet and cook until the tomatoes are thickened. Add the diced tomatoes and cook until heated through.

MAKES 4 TO 6 SERVINGS

Candied Sweet Potatoes

You can order Thanksgiving dinner every day at the Dutch Kitchen—turkey, of course, or ham. And what Thanksgiving dinner is complete without candied sweet potatoes?

6	sweet potatoes, peeled and sliced
3	tablespoons butter
½	cup packed brown sugar
½	teaspoon salt
1¼	cups hot water

Preheat the oven to 350°F. Arrange the sweet potato slices in a 2-quart baking dish. Mix together the butter, brown sugar, salt, and hot water. Pour the mixture over the potatoes. Tightly cover the dish with foil and bake for 40 minutes. Uncover and continue baking for 30 minutes longer or until the potatoes are tender.

MAKES 8 SERVINGS

Mashed Potatoes

The Dutch Kitchen is proud to report that its mashed potatoes are made fresh many times throughout the day. Tom explained that consistently good mashed potatoes aren't so simple to provide because the potatoes come from different parts of the country at different times of the year. Because potatoes vary in starchiness, the recipe must be subtly adjusted so they're always just right on the side of a turkey dinner.

2	pounds potatoes, peeled and sliced
3	tablespoons butter
⅓	cup hot milk
1	teaspoon salt
	Dash of black pepper

Cook the potatoes in boiling, salted water for 20 minutes or until tender; drain. Mash the potatoes in a mixer. Add the butter, milk, salt, and pepper and whip until light and creamy. Serve hot.

MAKES 6 TO 8 SERVINGS

Scalloped Potatoes

It is said that the old-time Pennsylvania Dutchman ate potatoes three times a day; and every time a cook made some, she'd make extra so there would be potatoes left over to fry the next day. Here's a good recipe for creamy, cheesy potatoes that go with any meat. But just because you serve them is no reason not to also have another starch on the table, such as sweet potatoes.

6	*potatoes, peeled and sliced*
½	*cup (1 stick) butter*
½	*cup all-purpose flour*
1	*small onion, chopped*
8	*cups half-and-half*
3	*cups grated sharp white cheese*

Preheat the oven to 350°F. In a greased 9 x 13-inch baking dish arrange the potato slices. In a medium saucepan melt the butter and whisk in the flour. Add the onion and cook until tender. Add the half-and-half and cheese. Cook on medium heat until the cheese is melted. Pour this mixture over the potatoes. Cover the baking dish with foil and bake for 1 hour.

MAKES 12 SERVINGS

Pennsylvania Dutch Filling (Stuffing)

What much of the rest of the world knows as stuffing or dressing is called filling in Pennsylvania Dutch country. Some recipes contain mashed potatoes in addition to the bread, but this one is more traditional. And it is filling.

1	medium onion, chopped
½	cup (1 stick) butter
2	cups chopped celery
4	cups water
1	loaf bread, cubed
1	tablespoon dried parsley
1	teaspoon dried thyme

Preheat the oven to 350°F. In a saucepan sauté the onion in the butter. Add the celery and cook until tender. Put the water in a large bowl. Add the bread cubes, onion mixture, parsley, and thyme and mix well. Spoon the filling in a buttered 9 x 13-inch baking dish and bake for 1 hour.

MAKES 12 SERVINGS

Bleenies

Bleenies are Polish potato pancakes that are popular throughout Schuylkill County. You'll find them at church picnics, summer fairs, and, of course, at the Dutch Kitchen. They're great topped with sour cream or applesauce.

8	*potatoes, peeled and sliced*
1	*large onion*
3	*eggs*
2	*teaspoons salt*
2	*teaspoons baking powder*
1	*cup all-purpose flour*

Process the potatoes and onion in a food processor until finely grated. In a large mixing bowl beat the eggs well. Add the salt, baking powder, and flour; mix well. Add the potatoes and onion. With your hands form the mixture into patties. Fry the patties in a large lightly greased skillet over medium heat like you would pancakes. When the edges turn light brown, flip the patties and fry until cooked.

MAKES 12 SERVINGS

Halushki

Halushki is a Polish dish that is a hearty main course all by itself, but it makes an exceptionally good companion to a few lengths of kielbasa.

½   cup (1 stick) butter

4   tablespoons chicken stock

1   teaspoon salt

1   teaspoon black pepper

1   small head cabbage

2   cups Potpie Noodles (see page 139)

In a large saucepan melt the butter and add the chicken stock, salt, and pepper. Shred the cabbage and add to the saucepan, stirring to coat the cabbage well. Cook on medium heat until the cabbage is tender. Add the Potpie Noodles and cook until warm.

MAKES 8 SERVINGS

Parmesan Rice

Multicultural implications aside, this full-flavored rice is a natural companion for good Schuylkill County kielbasa.

½	cup chopped onion
2	tablespoons butter
1	(28-ounce) can crushed tomatoes, not drained
1	cup water
¾	cup long grain rice
½	cup dry white wine
2	teaspoons chicken base
2	to 3 dashes hot pepper sauce
¼	teaspoon black pepper
⅓	cup grated Parmesan cheese

In a saucepan over medium heat sauté the onion in the butter. Stir in the tomatoes, water, rice, wine, chicken base, hot pepper sauce, and pepper. Bring the mixture to a boil, stirring frequently. Cover the saucepan with a lid and reduce the heat to low. Let the mixture cook for 1 hour or until the rice is tender. Remove the pan from the heat and stir in the Parmesan cheese.

MAKES 8 SERVINGS

Baked Apples

What we like about a baked apple is that it's always the right thing to eat: good for breakfast, lunch, or supper or as dessert or a snack. Of course, serve it warm and maybe with a dollop of heavy cream or a scoop of ice cream for a wonderful treat.

6	*medium apples*
½	*cup sugar*
1	*tablespoon ground cinnamon*
½	*cup (1 stick) chilled butter, chopped*

Preheat the oven to 350°F. Peel, core, and slice the apples. Place them in a large mixing bowl with the sugar, cinnamon, and butter. Mix gently. Place the apples in a greased 9 x 13-inch baking dish and bake for 1 hour.

MAKES 12 SERVINGS

Shredded Lemon Pepper Cabbage

If you are looking for a bright, zesty side dish to accompany a meat-and-potatoes meal, this cool, tart cabbage fills the bill. We especially like it alongside a ham steak or pork chop.

1	small head of cabbage
4	lemons
2	teaspoons salt
½	cup olive oil
1	teaspoon pepper

Remove the core of the cabbage and discard. Cut the head of cabbage into four pieces. Shred the cabbage with a medium grate. In a separate bowl juice the lemons and remove the seeds. Pour the lemon juice over the shredded cabbage. Add the salt, olive oil, and pepper to the cabbage. Mix well and serve cold as a side dish.

MAKES 6 TO 8 SERVINGS

· LUNCH ·

Gourmet Grilled Cheese

Egg Salad

Garden Egg Salad

Turkey Salad

Ham Salad

Tuna Salad

Hot Meatloaf Sandwich

Marinated Wimpy Burgers

Beef BBQ Sandwich

Pork BBQ Sandwich

Tom's Famous Grilled
Roast Beef & Swiss Sandwich

Pulled London Broil BBQ

Gourmet Grilled Cheese

If it's raining in Frackville, you can be sure the Dutch Kitchen will be serving these grilled cheese sandwiches with Cream of Tomato Soup on the side.

1	*(16-ounce) frozen white bread loaf*
4	*tablespoons butter*
4	*slices mozzarella cheese*
4	*slices Swiss cheese*
4	*slices red onion*
4	*slices tomato*

Place the frozen bread loaf in a greased 5 x 9-inch loaf pan. Place in a warm, still area and allow the loaf to rise for approximately 4½ hours. At a point just prior to baking the bread, preheat the oven to 350°F. Place the bread in the middle of the oven and bake for 20 minutes or until golden brown. Remove the bread from the oven and allow it to cool. Preheat a griddle or large fry pan to 350°F. Not counting the two end slices, slice the loaf into eight 1-inch thick slices. Butter one side of each bread slice and place the buttered side down on the hot griddle surface. Lay 1 slice of the mozzarella cheese, swiss cheese, red onion, and tomato on top of the bread. Top with a second slice of bread, buttered side up. Allow the sandwich to cook to a golden brown while melting the cheese inside. Flip the sandwich over to cook the other side.

MAKES 4 LARGE SANDWICHES

Variation: In order to save time, visit the local bakery and purchase a good quality, freshly baked bread that you can slice yourself.

Egg Salad

This recipe makes a gentle-flavored egg salad. If you like it spicier, up the amount of mustard or use high-quality Hungarian paprika.

5	hard-cooked eggs
¾	cup mayonnaise
½	teaspoon Dijon mustard
¼	teaspoon salt
¼	teaspoon black pepper
¼	teaspoon paprika

Peel and dice the eggs and place them in a medium mixing bowl with the mayonnaise, Dijon mustard, salt, pepper, and paprika. Mix just enough to blend.

MAKES 6 SERVINGS

Garden Egg Salad

For many people who love the flavor of egg salad, its drawback is a monotonous texture. Here's one fine solution: the crunch (and flavor) of fresh vegetables.

5	hard-cooked eggs
¾	cup mayonnaise
¼	teaspoon salt
¼	teaspoon black pepper
2	tablespoons shredded carrot
2	tablespoons diced green bell pepper
1	tablespoon diced red onion

Peel and dice the eggs and place them in a medium mixing bowl with the mayonnaise, salt, pepper, carrot, green pepper, and onion. Mix just enough to blend.

MAKES 6 SERVINGS

Turkey Salad

Use, skinless turkey in this recipe. All white meat is fine if you want a luncheonette-style salad, but use dark meat for more succulence.

2	cups chopped cooked turkey
1	cup diced celery
1	cup mayonnaise
1	teaspoon salt
1	teaspoon celery seed
½	teaspoon black pepper

In a medium mixing bowl combine the turkey, celery, mayonnaise, salt, celery seed, and pepper. Mix just enough to blend.

MAKES 8 SERVINGS

Ham Salad

It's amazing how good ham salad can be if you use good sweet pepper relish. This salad is particularly good in a sandwich with slices of Swiss or American cheese.

2	cups diced ham
1	cup diced celery
1	hard-cooked egg, diced
½	cup sweet pepper relish
1	cup mayonnaise
1	teaspoon salt
½	teaspoon black pepper

In a medium mixing bowl combine the ham, celery, egg, relish, mayonnaise, salt, and pepper. Mix just enough to blend.

MAKES 8 SERVINGS

Tuna Salad

Years ago, a luncheonette cook told us that the secret of good tuna salad, other than using good-quality tuna, is to use a common table fork to barely mix it—just enough to blend the ingredients, but not to pulverize anything.

2	cups white albacore tuna fish in water (about four 6-ounce cans)
1	cup mayonnaise
1	cup diced celery
1	teaspoon salt
½	teaspoon black pepper

Drain the liquid from the canned tuna and put the tuna in a medium mixing bowl. Add the mayonnaise, celery, salt, and pepper. Mix just enough to blend.

MAKES 8 SERVINGS

Hot Meatloaf Sandwich

Like turkey, meatloaf is a meal that enjoys a spectacular afterlife as hot-sandwich leftovers. While it isn't necessary to serve it with mashed potatoes on the side, the gravy-topped delight looks especially right on a plate with a gravy-topped volcano of creamy spuds.

4	*slices fresh white bread*
2	*cups beef gravy (see page 158)*
4	*slices meatloaf (see page 162)*

Place one piece of bread on a plate. Pour ½ cup warm beef gravy over the slice of bread. Place 2 pieces of warm meatloaf on top of the gravy. Top it off with another slice of bread. Pour another ½ cup of gravy on top of the sandwich to cover the bread. Repeat with the remaining ingredients to make the other sandwich.

MAKES 2 SANDWICHES

HEX SIGNS

This front-door hex is a friendly greeting.

Circular signs in brilliant colors festoon buildings throughout the farmland of eastern Pennsylvania. About the size of a large plate or platter, they appear on barn walls, above kitchen doors, and in vestibules of restaurants and motel lobbies.

The ornamental symbols are known as hex signs, but not because they are supposed to deliver a hex to evil spirits or cast spells upon passersby. Like the term Pennsylvania *Dutch*, which has nothing to do with the Netherlands, *hex* is an Americanized pronunciation of the German word *sechs*, meaning six, and referring to the six-pointed stars that were popular on the decorative signs put up by the original Deutsch farmers who settled this land some three centuries ago. They are, in fact, "six signs."

Original hex signs, painted by hand on wood, are now prized folk-art collectibles. During World War II, a Pennsylvania Dutchman named Jacob Zook introduced the process of applying colors to a circular board using silk screens, thus enabling the local populace to produce the signs faster than ever before. Still, each was made by an expert craftsman, and even these early semimass-produced signs are sought-after collectibles. Nowadays, newly-made hex signs are available on wood or cardboard at prices any tourist can afford.

While given no authority of magic power, most hex signs do convey specific meanings. A motif of tulips symbolizes faith, stars are for good luck, birds are signs of happiness, and hearts mean love. There are even hex signs specifically made to go near the front door with the word *Wilkum* to make strangers feel at home, while others say *Bless This House* and are popular indoors in kitchens. Colors are significant, too. Blue is supposed to convey a sense of security and protection to the dwelling, green means abundance of healthy soil, and red is an expression of powerful emotions. Some hex signs are more abstract, made in pleasing colors and geometric patterns. These, too, are known by their purpose to those who post them: "Just for pretty."

Marinated Wimpy Burgers

Wimpy, you might like to know, was Popeye's pal. He was a fatso who loved hamburgers. Hence the name of this Dutch Kitchen lunchtime favorite: hand-formed burgers, marinated and stewed in beef stock and served up on a fresh roll. Life is good.

---

6   *(4- to 6-ounce) ground sirloin burger patties*

4   *cups seasoned beef stock*

2   *large onions, sliced into ¼-inch-thick rings*

1   *tablespoon grated Parmesan cheese*

¼   *cup ketchup*

Start with 6 of your favorite hamburgers already cooked and just waiting for your party to begin. In a medium saucepan heat the beef stock over medium heat. Add the onion slices, Parmesan cheese, and ketchup. Cook until the onion rings become tender and then transfer the mixture to a slow cooker or electric Dutch oven set to medium heat (200°F). Add the burgers and heat for at least 2 hours prior to serving.

MAKES SIX (4- TO 6-OUNCE) BURGERS

Note: The beef stock can be made from a reserved roasting beef stock or from a prepackaged beef bouillon base.

Beef BBQ Sandwich

In much of America outside the South and Southwest, barbecued beef means ground meat that is flavored with a sweet tomato sauce . . . what some might know as a Sloppy Joe.

1	pound ground meat
½	cup ketchup
2	tablespoons chili sauce
1	small onion, diced
1	small green bell pepper, finely diced
1	tablespoon Worcestershire sauce
1	teaspoon white vinegar
1	tablespoon brown sugar
6	kaiser rolls

In a medium saucepan brown the ground meat. Drain, discarding three-fourths of the fat. Add the ketchup, chili sauce, onion, green pepper, Worcestershire, vinegar, and brown sugar. Simmer on low heat for 30 minutes. Serve on a fresh roll.

MAKES 6 SANDWICHES

Pork BBQ Sandwich

While this is the same recipe as that for Beef BBQ, it is amazing how dissimilar the two dishes are. This has less to do with taste than texture. Velvet-soft shredded pork makes a completely different impression on the tongue from that of chunky ground beef.

1½	*pounds seasoned pork roast, cooked and shredded*
½	*cup ketchup*
2	*tablespoons chili sauce*
1	*small onion, diced*
1	*small green bell pepper, finely diced*
1	*tablespoon Worcestershire sauce*
1	*teaspoon garlic salt*
1	*teaspoon white vinegar*
1	*tablespoon brown sugar*
6	*kaiser rolls*

Place the pork in a medium saucepan. Add the ketchup, chili sauce, onion, green pepper, Worcestershire, garlic salt, vinegar, and brown sugar. Simmer on low heat for about 30 minutes. Serve on a fresh roll.

MAKES 6 SANDWICHES

Tom's Famous Grilled Roast Beef & Swiss Sandwich

Top-notch ingredients make all the difference in Tom's famous sandwich. You want good bakery rye bread with a rugged crust (we prefer a seeded rye) and moist, rare roast beef. Use sweet Vidalia onions, and don't skimp on the butter. Please pass the mustard!

2	thinly sliced onion slices
1	plus 2 tablespoons butter
6	to 8 ounces tender roast beef, sliced thin
4	slices hard sour rye bread
4	slices Swiss cheese

In a skillet over medium heat, sauté the onion in 1 tablespoon butter. When the onion is tender, place the roast beef in the skillet to heat. Butter the rye bread (edge to edge) and place the buttered side down. Add the Swiss cheese slices onto each slice of rye bread and grill until the bread is light brown and the cheese melts. Lay the roast beef and onions on top of the cheese. Cover with the other slice of grilled rye bread.

MAKES 2 SANDWICHES

Pulled London Broil BBQ

Nearly every good cook from every region of the country has a special way with hot beef sandwiches. We like the Dutch Kitchen version because the meat is pot-roast tender and pulled from the roast in big soft hunks. Sturdy rolls are essential, but even the most muscular Kaiser roll will eventually disintegrate from the beef juices that sop it.

1	(2- to 4-pound) sirloin, London Broil cut
⅓	cup beef stock
½	cup BBQ sauce (see page 40)
6	to 8 Kaiser rolls

Preheat the oven to 250°F. Place the sliced sirloin into a small roasting pan with a wire rack base. Add the beef stock and cover the pan. Place it in the oven for 3½ hours or until well done. Remove the sirloin from the oven and let it cool to the point that it can be easily handled. Reserve the stock for later use. Place the beef onto a cutting board, use a roasting fork to pull the sirloin apart and add it to the reserved beef stock. Add the BBQ sauce and blend well. Reheat if necessary. Serve warm on a Kaiser roll.

MAKES 6 TO 8 SANDWICHES

• DINNER •

Cheese & Potato Pierogies

Shepherd's Pie

Chicken Pie

Turkey Potpie
with Noodles

Potpie Noodles

Deviled Crab Cakes

Salmon Croquettes

Roast Turkey

Turkey Gravy

Turkey Croquettes

Halupkis

Roast Pork Tenderloin
& Sauerkraut

Stuffed Pork Chops

Ham with Cabbage
& Potatoes

Corned Beef & Cabbage
with Potatoes

Pepper Steak

Simple Beef Chuck Roast

Beef Gravy

Salisbury Steak

Stuffed Green Peppers

Beef Burgundy

Meatloaf

Ham Loaf

Beef Stroganoff

Meat Pinwheels

Beer Battered Fish

Meatballs

Breaded Center Cut Pork Chops

Simple Beef Eye Roast

Pineapple Glazed Ham

Cheese & Potato Pierogies

Pierogies are Eastern European — Polish in particular — but in the eastern heartland they have become an all-American dish. A few of them are a nice appetizer and a bowlful is a meal. Their onion and butter sauce exudes one of the world's great kitchen aromas.

FILLING:

6   *medium potatoes, peeled and quartered*

1   *quart (4 cups) water*

¾   *cup grated American cheese*

½   *teaspoon salt*

DOUGH:

2   *cups all-purpose flour*

2   *eggs*

½   *teaspoon salt*

     Lukewarm water

SAUCE:

¼   *cup (½ stick) butter*

2   *medium onions, chopped*

For the filling, combine the potatoes and water in a medium saucepan and bring to a boil. Once the potatoes are tender, remove from the heat and drain. Mash the potatoes until smooth and add the cheese and salt.

In a mixing bowl combine the flour, eggs, salt, and enough water to make workable dough. Flour your rolling surface and roll the dough out to a ⅛-inch thickness. Cut into 2-inch squares. Place some of the filling in the center of each square. Fold the dough over and pinch the corners to seal the edges. Drop the pierogies into boiling water and cook them for 6 minutes or until they float.

For the sauce, melt the butter in a small saucepan and sauté the onions until tender. Pour the sauce over the finished pierogies.

MAKES 4 SERVINGS

Shepherd's Pie

Traditional shepherd's pie is made with lamb, but the Dutch Kitchen's version is a beef bonanza. With its crusty-topped mashed potatoes, it is a one-dish meal supreme.

1	pound ground beef
¼	cup chopped onion
¼	cup chopped green bell pepper
2	cups beef stock
2	tablespoons butter
2	tablespoons all-purpose flour
1	teaspoon salt
1	teaspoon dried thyme
2	cups frozen mixed vegetables
4	cups mashed potatoes
2	teaspoons paprika

Brown the ground beef in a large skillet with the onion and green pepper. Add the beef stock. In a small saucepan melt the butter over low heat and whisk in the flour. Add this mixture to the beef stock to thicken. Stir in the salt, thyme, and mixed vegetables. Let it simmer for 20 minutes. Preheat the broiler. Spoon the mixture into an ovenproof casserole dish. Top it with the mashed potatoes, using a large pastry bag if desired. Sprinkle the paprika on top. Place the pie under the broiler to brown.

MAKES 6 TO 8 SERVINGS

Chicken Pie

Do not confuse chicken pie with chicken potpie. This is the version more familiar to most eaters, made in a crust rather than with the soft noodles of a potpie. Tom says, "In our opinion, both are equally delicious."

1	*cup chopped stewed chicken*
1	*small onion, chopped*
1	*teaspoon salt*
½	*teaspoon black pepper*
1	*(10-ounce) bag frozen mixed vegetables*
2	*hard-cooked eggs, chopped*
2	*tablespoons chopped fresh parsley*
½	*cup chicken stock*
2	*uncooked piecrusts (see page 173)*

Preheat the oven to 425°F. In a medium bowl combine the chicken, onion, salt, pepper, vegetables, eggs, parsley, and chicken stock. Stir gently. Spoon the mixture into 1 piecrust. Top with the second piecrust and pinch the edges. Bake in the oven for about 15 minutes and then reduce the heat to 375°F and bake for 45 minutes.

MAKES 1 (9-INCH) PIE

Turkey Potpie with Noodles

On a serious Pennsylvania Dutch supper table, where hard-working diners are looking for maximum calorie intake, potpie is just one of several main-course dishes. For most of us it is a full meal unto itself. In order to keep everyone smiling, veteran cook Billy Horan is kept busy preparing our potpie on a weekly basis.

8	cups turkey or chicken stock
1	cup diced carrots
½	cup diced onion
1	cup chopped celery
1	teaspoon black pepper
½	tablespoon salt
1	teaspoon dried thyme
3	cups cooked turkey pieces
4	medium potatoes, cubed
½	cup (1 stick) butter
½	cup all-purpose flour
	Potpie noodles (see next page)

In a large stockpot combine the turkey stock, carrots, onion, celery, black pepper, salt, and thyme and bring to a simmer. Just before the vegetables are tender, add the turkey pieces and potatoes. Let the mixture simmer for 20 more minutes or until the potatoes are tender. Meanwhile, heat the butter in a skillet over medium. Stir in the flour to make a roux. Stir the roux into the simmering soup a little at a time to thicken. Remove the pot from the heat, stir in the potpie noodles, and serve.

MAKES 8 SERVINGS

Potpie Noodles

First-time visitors to this part of Pennsylvania often are confused over the term potpie. Somehow, the rest of the nation thinks of potpie as a pie with a crust that pockets chicken or turkey and vegetables. Here, potpie is a kind of stew featuring thick, soft noodles.

1	cup all-purpose flour
¼	teaspoon salt
½	teaspoon baking powder
1	egg
1	tablespoon butter
¼	cup water

In a medium mixing bowl combine the flour, salt, and baking powder. Stir to blend. Beat the egg and add it to the flour mixture. Melt the butter and add it slowly to the flour mixture. Add the water and mix gently with a fork. With your hands gently knead the dough. Place the dough on a floured surface and roll it out with a rolling pin. Cut the noodles into 2-inch squares. Drop them into boiling water to cook. The noodles are ready when they float to the top.

MAKES ENOUGH NOODLES FOR 6 TO 8 SERVINGS OF POTPIE

Deviled Crab Cakes

It's not so surprising that deviled crab cakes are popular throughout so much of eastern Pennsylvania when you consider that the Chesapeake Bay isn't all that far away. Cooks here love to embellish, enrich, and liberally spice so much of what they make. These luscious cakes are a perfect example.

½   cup (1 stick) butter

1   cup diced celery

1   small onion, peeled and diced

1   small green bell pepper, diced

1   tablespoon yellow mustard

1   tablespoon Worcestershire sauce

½   cup chopped fresh parsley

1   pound lump crabmeat

2   eggs, well beaten

2   hard-cooked eggs, diced

1   plus 1 cups breadcrumbs

Melt the butter in a medium saucepan. Sauté the celery, onion, and green pepper until tender. Add the mustard and Worcestershire sauce. Transfer the mixture to a large mixing bowl and add the parsley, crabmeat, and beaten eggs. Mix well with your hands. Fold in the hard-cooked eggs and 1 cup of the breadcrumbs. Preheat the broiler. Mold the crab mixture into crab cakes and arrange on a baking sheet. Sprinkle with the remaining 1 cup breadcrumbs. Broil for 20 to 25 minutes.

MAKES 12 CRAB CAKES

Note: To deep-fry these, beat 2 eggs with ½ cup milk. Roll the crab cakes in this mixture and then roll them in 1 cup breadcrumbs. Fry them in a skillet in hot oil until light brown an both sides.

Salmon Croquettes

A lunchtime favorite at the Dutch Kitchen, salmon croquettes are especially wonderful when drizzled with Lemony Dill Sauce (see page 41).

½	cup (1 stick) butter
2	cups diced celery
1	small green bell pepper, chopped
1	small onion, peeled and diced
1	cup finely shredded carrots
3	cups shredded poached salmon
1	cup mashed potatoes
1	cup heavy whipping cream
1	cup water
½	cup all-purpose flour
2	eggs, well beaten
½	cup milk
2	cups finely grated breadcrumbs

Heat the butter in a small skillet and sauté the celery, green pepper, onion, and carrots. In a large mixing bowl combine the salmon and mashed potatoes. Mix well. Transfer the vegetable mixture to a medium stockpot. Stir in the whipping cream, water, and flour and cook until thickened. Add to the salmon and mashed potatoes. Mix well. Mold into croquettes. (We use a conical disher to shape the croquettes, but if you don't have one you can use an ice cream scoop.) Mix the eggs and milk together in a small bowl. Roll the croquettes in the milk mixture and then in the breadcrumbs to coat. Deep-fry in a skillet to cook. If desired, top with Lemony-Dill Sauce.

MAKES 6 SERVINGS

PEOPLE OF THE DUTCH KITCHEN

Michelle and John Morgan

One way to define a great Roadfood restaurant is by how well it reflects good people's passions and personalities. Nowhere is that more true than the Dutch Kitchen, where excellence is all about the family that has run it for some thirty years and the staff who have been with them, in some cases, from the beginning.

John Morgan opened the Dutch Kitchen in 1971. John grew up in Frackville but moved away as a young man because the slumping coal business hit the town hard. He worked in retail and then moved back to town in the late 1960s, helping his parents at their auto supply store. When the interstate was completed in 1967, John began to pay attention to a building lot near the highway. In horse-and-buggy days, the lot had been home to the Valley House Hotel, a way station for travelers along Schuylkill County's dirt turnpike. But it had been empty for decades, and John couldn't help but take note of the fact that a lot of people would get off at the new highway exit and search in vain for something to eat.

John's idea to open a restaurant in Frackville wasn't totally out of the blue. He had experience in food service at the lunch counters of Grant's stores, and his wife's family had always been involved with cafés and bakeries in the area. "Frackville isn't a big town," he says. "Population 5,500. But you take all the little patches around and that number goes up to 100,000. [*Patch* is coal-country lingo for a small community of homes around the coal breaker.] From the beginning, we wanted this restaurant to be the community's place as well as one for people passing through. It wasn't long after we opened that the Dutch Kitchen became a gathering spot for families after funerals and for rehearsal dinners, and to celebrate christenings, anniversaries, and birthdays." John's wife, Michelle, added to the character of the dining room by filling it with Pennsylvania crafts from Dutch country and beyond.

Jennifer and Tom Levkulic in a rare moment of relaxation at a table in the vintage diner.

The Morgans' daughter Jennifer did not intend to go into the family business. She studied psychology in school and has a master's degree in education. "Restaurants get in your blood," Jen says. "When dad turned fifty, he started to think about selling the Dutch Kitchen. I knew I didn't want that to happen. I had virtually grown up here, and when I was twenty-five, I started work full time." That was 1993.

In the late 1990s, Jennifer's husband Tom Levkulic, a Pottsville native, was running his own company as an environmental consultant. Tom recalls, "We were expecting our first son, so Jen was home pulling her hair out about how they needed a new manager at the restaurant now that she would have to take a maternity leave. I've always loved to cook—soups, especially—so I came on board." Although Tom and Jen pretty much run the place, John Morgan never did walk away. Tom jokes, "John wants to be fired, but we won't do it. He's too valuable to the business in all kinds of ways. For one thing, he is obsessed with cleaning. So he not only runs things, he also wipes the walls."

Tom is the first to tell you how vital the enduring staff has been to the restaurant's well-being. "Annie, Rosie, Joyce," he says, naming some of the veteran waitstaff, "they are icons. We have so many in the kitchen and on the floor who have been here for years and know all the ropes. I think one of the reasons they stay is that my father-in-law believes in taking good care of his staff: flexible schedules, health insurance, paid

143

vacations . . . and of course, when you work here, you eat well!"

One of the favorite staff-loyalty stories told by those who work at the Dutch Kitchen is about the time Rosie the waitress woke to find her house on fire. As she and her husband were running out to safety, he paused to remind her not to escape without her waitress shoes. He knew that no matter what happened at home, she'd want to go to work.

Rosie is one of several staff members who are as much a defining part of the Dutch Kitchen experience as chicken potpie. In a business notorious for employee turnover, this restaurant is extraordinary for the number of employees who are in their second, and in some cases *third*, decade of service.

Bill Horan, who has worked in the kitchen over twenty years, says that one of the joys of being here a long time is seeing regular customers every week or, in some cases, once in the spring and once in the fall. "We have people who travel from Canada to Florida every year," he explains. "We are marked on their map. A pair of brothers named Adam and Evan come to mind," Bill says. "Their family drove

Chef Billy Horan has been a member of the kitchen staff for more than twenty years.

through town twice each year, and on each visit the boys would come tap on the kitchen door. They wanted to see what I was doing in there. So I'd show them around, and they loved it. Now they're adults, but they still tap on the door when they pass through." Bill describes his job in the kitchen as "some of everything, this and that: chow-chow, potpies, sugar cookies." Every night when he leaves at about ten, he puts the turkeys in the oven to slow-roast all night. By the time he comes in at mid-day, they are perfect.

Joyce Gallagher, who started as a day-shift waitress in 1981 and is now the restaurant manager and hostess, delights in telling about the camaraderie of the staff during the blizzard of 1993. "The whole town was closed. People who had pulled off the interstate were stuck here in the motels because the snow was higher than their cars; travel was impossible. Bill and I lived close enough that we were able to walk to work. It was us and any locals we could grab to help out in the kitchen. We managed to open the place, and the dining room was full. People had no place else to go. The town maintenance men went by the home of Joyce Hereshko (waitress since 1973) and carried her to work in the bucket of an overhead loader— just about dumped her here in the parking lot! Afterwards, the *Pottsville Republican* awarded her the Golden Shovel for her perseverance. But I tell you, Billy (Horan) should have gotten one, too." Joyce Gallagher agrees

Joyce Gallagher started as a day-shift waitress in 1981 and is now the Dutch Kitchen's manager and hostess.

with Bill that the continuity of seeing children grow up is a priceless fringe benefit of long-time employment at the Dutch Kitchen. "We are more than just a restaurant to our regular customers. For some of the kids who come in here, we are like psychologists and advisers. Sometimes it can be a tricky situation because they tell us things they wouldn't tell their parents. What do we do with that information?" Joyce's favorite funny moment is the time a family made reservations for a funeral dinner. Because they didn't want to spend money on a limousine to transport the urn with ashes of the deceased from the funeral home back to Frackville, they had the cremated remains shipped via common carrier. "It got lost!" Joyce says with some alarm, reporting that the funeral dinner was an awkward one indeed.

A big booster of Schuylkill County, Joyce brags that it once contained the most heavily populated square mile in the United States. "Because of the mines," she explains. She also notes that the Dorsey Brothers were from over in Shenandoah ("One of them is buried in the cemetery there") and that Jack Palance is from up in Hazelton.

Thirty-year veteran waitress Joyce Hereshko is known for kibbitzing with customers.

John Morgan likes to remember the time Palance bought a bunch of souvenirs off the wall after having a meal here. "Shaking hands with him is like shaking hands with a bear," he says. "He told me he still does one hundred push-ups every day, and I remember him saying, 'Gettin' old ain't for sissies.'"

Thirty-year veteran waitress Joyce Hereshko sat down and wrote a two-page memo for us listing all the celebrities she remembers from her tenure at the restaurant. The list, in Joyce's words, includes:

- *Three Dog Night*
- *Joe Kennedy, Jr.*
- *Some Denver Broncos*
- *Rick Springsteen*
- *Brenda Lee*
- *Willie Nelson*
- *A Harlem Globetrotter on his way to Hershey*
- *Joe Gibbs, Washington Redskin coach*
- *Anna Lee on the way to White Haven*
- *Producers and Directors from Germany making a movie about Centralia*

- *Charlie Prose*
- *Jerry Vale*
- *Uncle Ted from The Munsters*
- *Karen Harch, Anchorwoman, Newscenter 16*
- *Marissa Burke, Newscenter 16*
- *Mike Stevens, "On the Road," Newscenter 16*
- *The Real Tall Girl from Channel 2 or 3*

Roast Turkey

A roast turkey dinner is never humdrum. It evokes Sunday supper, holiday banquets, and family get-togethers. And for those of us in search of Roadfood, it has become a signature dish of the Dutch Kitchen—on the menu every day.

5	tablespoons softened butter
1	tablespoon chopped fresh thyme
1	tablespoon chopped fresh rosemary
½	teaspoon salt
½	teaspoon black pepper
1	(15- to 18-pound) turkey
4	cups chicken stock
1	large onion, chopped extra coarsely

Preheat the oven to 350°F. In a small mixing bowl combine the butter, thyme, and rosemary, salt, and pepper. Place the turkey on a rack inside a large roasting pan. Rub the herb butter on the outside as well as the inside of the bird. Starting at the neck end, carefully separate the skin from the breast of the bird. Using about one-third of the herb butter, butter the breast area under the skin. Using the remaining herb butter, butter the outside of the bird. The turkey can now be stuffed using your favorite bread stuffing recipe. Close the stuffing cavity with either roasting pins or roasting cord. Add the chicken stock and chopped onion to the roasting pan and place the turkey in the oven. Allow 25 to 30 minutes of cooking time per pound. Once the turkey is done, remove from the oven and allow to rest for 30 minutes before carving.

MAKES 12 TO 15 SERVINGS

Turkey Gravy

Genuine turkey gravy is essential for a supper of sliced turkey, filling (stuffing), and mashed potatoes; but it also is a necessary part of lunch the next day. No hot turkey sandwich is complete without a generous blanket of gravy.

2	cups turkey stock
1	teaspoon salt
½	teaspoon black pepper
¼	cup (½ stick) butter
½	cup all-purpose flour

Make the turkey stock from the drippings after roasting a turkey. Pour the drippings into a large measuring cup. Try to include any and all scrapings or browned bits that have adhered to the roasting pan. Once the drippings have settled, remove and discard the fat that has risen to the top. If needed, add water to make 2 cups.

In a medium saucepan heat the turkey stock over medium-low heat and add the salt and pepper. Prepare a roux by melting the butter in a small saucepan over low heat and adding the flour, whisking well until smooth and thick. Once the turkey stock has reached a slow boil, slowly whisk in the roux mixture, being careful not to over thicken the gravy. Cook and stir for 2 minutes.

MAKES 2 CUPS

Turkey Croquettes

Hail the croquette! For many years, croquettes were out of fashion among American cooks, although a handful of tradition-minded diners and tearooms kept the tradition alive. Recently the croquette has had a comeback, not only in diners and cafés, but in swanky restaurants, too. A well-made croquette, topped with good gravy, is a vividly flavored legacy of kitchens long ago.

½ cup (1 stick) butter

2 cups diced celery

1 small green bell pepper, diced

1 small onion, diced

1 cup finely shredded carrots

3 cups chopped turkey meat

1 cup water

2 cups heavy whipping cream

½ cup all-purpose flour

2 eggs, well beaten

½ cup milk

2 cups finely ground breadcrumbs

In a small skillet heat the butter over medium heat and sauté the celery, green pepper, onion, and carrots. Place the turkey in a pot, cover with water, and bring to a full boil. Let the turkey cool a bit before draining. Run the turkey through a meat grinder or finely chop it by hand with a chef's knife. In a large pot combine the vegetable mixture, water, whipping cream, and flour and cook until thickened. Transfer the mixture to large mixing bowl and add the turkey. Mix well and form into croquettes. (We use a conical disher to shape the croquettes, but if you don't have one, you can use an ice cream scoop.) Mix the eggs and the milk in a small bowl. Roll the croquettes in the milk mixture and then in the breadcrumbs to coat. Deep-fry in a skillet to cook. Top with turkey gravy.

MAKES 6 SERVINGS

Halupkis

It isn't necessary to be Polish to consider halupkis your soul food. Like Pierogies (see page 135), they are an old-world dish that has become a staple on menus throughout the region.

1	gallon (16 cups) plus ¼ cup water
1	large head cabbage
1	pound lean ground meat
1½	cups cooked rice
1	teaspoon salt
1	teaspoon black pepper
1	(46-ounce) can tomato juice
½	cup ketchup
1	tablespoon ham base or bouillon cube

In a large stockpot bring 1 gallon of the water to a boil. Deeply core the cabbage head and remove any spoiled outer leaves. Once the water boils, submerge the cabbage into the stockpot, making sure the water gets into the core cavity. While cooking, carefully remove any tender leaves that begin to fall away from the head and set them aside to cool. Once all of the tender leaves have been removed, combine the ground meat and rice in a mixing bowl. Add the salt and pepper and mix well. Place a portion of the meat and rice mixture in the center of each cabbage leaf. Tuck the sides of the leaf over the filling and roll to enclose. Place each rolled halupki side by side tightly in a roasting pan. Preheat the oven to 350°F. In a large saucepan heat the tomato juice, ketchup, the remaining ¼ cup water, and ham base over low heat. Once the ham base or bouillon cube dissolves, pour the tomato mixture over the halupkis and place them in the oven. Bake them for 45 minutes.

MAKES 4 SERVINGS

Roast Pork Tenderloin & Sauerkraut

It is amazing how this two-note dish with a sprinkle of spice creates profound harmony on a dinner plate.

4	pounds pork tenderloin
½	teaspoon garlic salt
½	teaspoon black pepper
1	cup water
1	(16-ounce) can sauerkraut

Preheat the oven to 350°F. Rub the pork tenderloin with the garlic salt and pepper onto the outside of the loin top and bottom. Place the tenderloin in a roasting pan with the water and cover with foil. Cook for about 1½ hours. Remove the foil and add the sauerkraut to the roasting pan. Cook an additional 30 minutes.

MAKE 4 TO 6 SERVINGS

Stuffed Pork Chops

This recipe works with regular pork chops or smoked chops. Red onions are good. Sweet Vidalias are even better.

4	*double-cut pork chops with a pocket for stuffing*
¼	*cup Italian salad dressing*
2	*cups Pennsylvania Dutch Filling (see page 111)*
½	*teaspoon garlic salt*
½	*teaspoon black pepper*
1	*small red onion sliced into ¼-inch-thick rings*

Preheat the oven to 350°F. Place the chops in a small roasting pan or dish. Using a basting brush, coat the chops inside and out with the Italian dressing. Stuff the chops firmly with the Pennsylvania Dutch Filling and season them with the garlic salt and black pepper. Lay the onion rings on top of the chops and add a little water to the roasting pan. Cover with foil and bake for 35 minutes. Uncover and bake for 15 minutes longer.

MAKES 4 SERVINGS

Ham with Cabbage & Potatoes

Sounds simple, is simple; but this uncomplicated plate of food is one of the most delicious we've ever eaten at the Dutch Kitchen. With a run through the salad bar to begin, a block of cornbread on the side, and a piece of Shoofly Pie or Jewish Apple Cake for dessert, it is a not-to-be-forgotten feast.

12	*cups water*
2	*meaty smoked ham hocks*
1	*medium head cabbage, cored and quartered*
3	*potatoes, peeled and quartered*

In a large stockpot combine the water and ham hocks and boil for about 45 minutes. Remove the ham hocks once the meat becomes tender and pulls easily from the bone. Remove all the meat and dice it into bite-size pieces. Discard the bones, return the ham meat back to the stock and bring the mixture to a boil. Add the cabbage and cook until just about tender, 25 minutes. Add the potatoes and cook until tender. Remove from the heat and serve in a large bowl.

MAKES 4 SERVINGS

Corned Beef
& Cabbage with Potatoes

On St. Patty's day corned beef and cabbage is always served with slices of Jennifer's homemade Irish Soda Bread (see page 23).

4	pounds corned beef brisket
16	cups water
1	large head cabbage, quartered
4	potatoes, peeled and quartered

In a large stockpot submerge the brisket in the water and bring to a simmering boil for 4 hours or until a fork can penetrate the center easily. Just prior to completing the brisket cook time, add the cabbage and cook for 25 minutes. Add the potatoes. Once the potatoes are tender, remove the pot from the heat and let stand for 20 minutes before serving.

MAKES 6 SERVINGS

Pepper Steak

Red wine gives this pepper steak an intoxicating scent. If you simmer it long enough, the alcohol will cook off and its perfume and flavor will bond with the savory juices of the steak.

½	plus ¼ cup butter (1 ½ sticks total)
3	medium green bell peppers, sliced
3	medium onions, sliced
9	large mushrooms, sliced
1½	cups stock made from beef base
½	teaspoon salt
¼	teaspoon black pepper
3	pounds beef tenderloin, sliced
½	cup all-purpose flour
6	tablespoons red Burgundy wine

In a large saucepan melt ½ cup of the butter and sauté the peppers, onions, and mushrooms for 6 to 8 minutes. Add the beef stock and simmer for 10 minutes. Season the tenderloin slices with the salt and pepper. Dip the slices in the flour and sauté them in the remaining ¼ cup butter in a skillet for 2 to 4 minutes. Add the tenderloin to the vegetables and simmer for 15 minutes. Add the wine and simmer for 3 minutes.

MAKES 4 TO 6 SERVINGS

Simple Beef Chuck Roast

Chuck roast is a meal that takes a lot of time but little effort. After three or four hours in a slow oven, sealed well inside its roasting pan, this meat will be ready to fall apart as soon as you touch it with a fork.

2	tablespoons oil
1	(5 to 7-pound) chuck roast
2	tablespoons all-purpose flour
2	medium onions, sliced
¼	teaspoon salt
¼	teaspoon black pepper
1	(6-ounce) can tomato paste

Preheat the oven to 300°F. Heat the oil in a large frying pan over medium-high heat. Lightly flour both sides of the roast and quickly sear it. Set aside the roast and transfer any remaining oil and cracklings to a roasting pan. Place the sliced onions in the bottom of the pan. Season both sides of the roast with salt and pepper and place it in the roasting pan on top of the sliced onions. Last, but not least, spread the top of the roast with the tomato paste. Tightly cover and roast for 3 to 4 hours.

MAKES 4 TO 6 SERVINGS

Beef Gravy

Once you've made and savored gravy made from the drippings of a roast beef, the stuff that comes in a can or jar will be anathema.

---

2   *cups beef stock*

1   *teaspoon salt*

½   *teaspoon black pepper*

¼   *cup (½ stick) butter*

½   *cup all-purpose flour*

After removing roasted beef from the roasting pan, pour the beef drippings into a large measuring cup. Try to include any and all scrapings or browned bits that have adhered to the roasting pan. Once the drippings have settled, remove and discard the fat that has risen to the top. If needed, add water to make 2 cups.

In a medium saucepan heat the beef stock and add the salt and pepper. Prepare a roux by melting the butter in a small saucepan over low heat and adding the flour, whisking well until smooth and thick. Once the beef stock has reached a slow boil, slowly whisk in the roux mixture, being careful not to over-thicken the gravy.

MAKES 2 CUPS

Salisbury Steak

Far more than a glorified hamburger, Salisbury steak actually was first created as a health food. Dr. J. H. Salisbury, a nineteenth-century British doctor, believed that the road to well being from almost any ailment was to eat plenty of beef. This muscular dish was named for him.

1	pound ground sirloin
½	cup finely chopped green bell peppers
1	small onion, finely chopped
2	tablespoons Worcestershire sauce
1	tablespoon A-1 sauce
1	teaspoon garlic salt
1	teaspoon black pepper
1	cup water
1	cup breadcrumbs

Preheat the oven to 350°F. In a large mixing bowl combine the ground sirloin, green peppers, onion, Worcestershire sauce, A-1 sauce, garlic salt, pepper, water, and breadcrumbs. Mix well with your hands. Form the mixture into four patties and arrange them in a baking dish. Bake them for 40 minutes. Top the steaks with Beef Gravy (see previous page).

MAKES 4 SERVINGS

Stuffed Green Peppers

A diner classic, these peppers are prepared as a frequent special at the Dutch Kitchen. The only trick to this uncomplicated recipe is to find green peppers that are stout and broad and balance well in the pan once they're stuffed.

1½	*pounds lean ground beef*
1½	*cups cooked rice*
1	*medium onion, finely chopped*
½	*cup ketchup*
1	*tablespoon Worcestershire sauce*
1	*teaspoon salt*
1	*teaspoon black pepper*
1	*(46-ounce) can tomato juice*
¼	*cup water*
1	*tablespoon ham base or bouillon cube*
8	*medium green bell peppers*

Preheat the oven to 350°F. In a medium frying pan brown the ground beef. Drain off excess oil and discard. In a mixing bowl combine the meat, rice, onion, ketchup, Worcestershire, salt, and pepper. In a large saucepan heat the tomato juice, water, and ham base over medium heat. When the tomato mixture is almost boiling, add it to the meat and vegetable mixture. Mix well with caution; the tomato juice is still hot. Cut off the tops of the green peppers and take out the seeds and membranes. Stand the peppers upright in a 9 x 13-inch casserole dish. Fill the peppers with the meat and rice mixture, pouring any remaining mixture in and around the peppers. Cover and bake for 45 minutes.

MAKES 8 SERVINGS

Variation: Add diced ham to the tomato stock and ham base.

Beef Burgundy

This is a dish loved by hungry travelers as well as weekend regulars who come to the Dutch Kitchen for home-style meals that stick to your ribs. We like it served atop a plateful of egg noodles glistening with butter.

1½	pounds beef cubes
3	cups Burgundy wine
2	plus 2 tablespoons butter
1	teaspoon salt
½	teaspoon black pepper
5	cups beef stock
1	small onion, cubed
1	cup chopped carrot
1	pound mushrooms, sliced
1	teaspoon dried thyme
2	tablespoons all-purpose flour

Marinate the beef cubes in the wine overnight. Preheat the oven to 300°F. Drain the wine from the beef cubes and reserve it for later. Sauté the beef cubes in 2 tablespoons of the butter in a large saucepan. Add the salt and pepper. Add the reserved wine, beef stock, onion, carrots, mushrooms, and thyme. Place in an oven-safe casserole dish and bake for 1½ hours. In a small saucepan melt the remaining 2 tablespoons butter and whisk in the flour until combined. Add to the beef mixture and stir until thickened as desired.

MAKES 6 SERVINGS

Note: This is great served over buttered egg noodles or rice.

Meatloaf

The Dutch Kitchen's all-beef meatloaf is dense and moist, but it wouldn't be complete without a blanket of gravy on top. And don't forget the mashed potatoes on the side.

1	pound ground sirloin
1	cup finely chopped celery
1	small onion, diced
2	eggs, well beaten
1	cup water
1	cup breadcrumbs
1	teaspoon salt
½	teaspoon black pepper
1	tablespoon Worcestershire sauce

Preheat the oven to 350°F. In a large mixing bowl combine the ground sirloin, celery, onion, eggs, water, breadcrumbs, salt, pepper, and Worcestershire sauce. Mix well with your hands. Mold into a loaf, place on a baking sheet, and bake for 50 minutes.

MAKES 6 SERVINGS

Ham Loaf

The smoky-sweet flavor of ham gives this loaf a character totally unlike the meatloaf made with beef or beef and pork. We love ham loaf with mashed or escalloped potatoes on the side.

1	pound smoked ham, ground
1	egg
½	cup breadcrumbs
¼	cup milk
¼	teaspoon ground cloves
¼	teaspoon salt
¼	teaspoon black pepper

Preheat the oven to 350°F. In a large mixing bowl combine the ground ham, egg, breadcrumbs, milk, cloves, salt, and pepper. Mix by hand and form into a loaf. Place the loaf on a baking sheet in the middle of the oven and bake uncovered for 1 hour.

MAKES 4 SERVINGS

Beef Stroganoff

Although its origins are Russian (named for Count Stroganov, a nineteenth-century diplomat), Beef Stroganoff has become a staple of diners and home cooks throughout the United States. While it is often served with rice or rice pilaf, the Dutch Kitchen's way is to bed it on buttered egg noodles.

1½	*pounds beef cubes*
4	*plus 2 tablespoons butter*
1	*teaspoon salt*
½	*teaspoon black pepper*
5	*cups beef stock*
1	*small onion, cubed*
1 ½	*cups sliced mushrooms*
¼	*teaspoon dried rosemary*
¼	*teaspoon dried marjoram*
¼	*teaspoon dried thyme*
4	*tablespoons all-purpose flour*
2	*cups sour cream*

Sauté the beef cubes in 4 tablespoons of the butter in a large stockpot over medium-high heat and add the salt and pepper. Add the beef stock, onion, mushrooms, rosemary, marjoram, and thyme. Simmer for 45 minutes. In a small saucepan make a roux by melting the remaining 2 tablespoons butter and whisking in the flour. Add the roux a little bit at a time to the Beef Stroganoff to thicken as desired. Remove from the heat and add the sour cream. Serve over buttered egg noodles.

MAKES 6 SERVINGS

Meat Pinwheels

Meat pinwheels are a kind of blue-collar beef Wellington: a felicitous combination of meat and bread accompanied by beef gravy. We suggest serving the gravy in a separate gravy boat so diners can admire the spiral effect of the dish before smothering it.

BISCUIT MIX:

2	cups all-purpose flour
1	tablespoon baking powder
½	teaspoon cream of tartar
¾	tablepoon sugar
¼	tablespoon salt
⅓	cup powdered milk
½	cup vegetable shortening
⅔	cup cold water

FILLING:

1	pound ground sirloin
1	small diced onion
	Salt and pepper

For the biscuit mix, in a large mixing bowl combine the flour, baking powder, cream of tartar, sugar, salt, and powdered milk and mix well. Cut in the shortening until the mixture resembles fine crumbs. Add the cold water to the crumbs and stir gently with a fork until combined. Form the dough into a ball with your hands and with a rolling pin roll the dough out to ½-inch thickness on a floured surface. Preheat the oven to 350°F.

For the filling, brown the ground sirloin in a skillet with the onion. Drain the grease and add the salt and pepper to taste. Spread the meat mixture thinly across the rolled-out biscuit dough. Roll the dough as you would a jelly roll. Cut it into 2-inch-thick servings and place them on a lightly greased baking sheet. Bake the pinwheels for 20 to 25 minutes. Serve with beef gravy.

MAKES 6 SERVINGS

Beer Battered Fish

You don't have to use Yuengling Beer in this recipe, but Schuylkill County aficionados of the brew from America's oldest brewery swear that they can taste the difference.

5	eggs
2	cups beer (we prefer Yuengling)
3	cups milk
3	cups all-purpose flour
1½	teaspoons salt
½	teaspoon crushed red pepper
1	teaspoon baking powder
½	teaspoon Old Bay seasoning
8	medium white haddock fillets

In a large mixing bowl beat the eggs. Add the beer and milk and mix well. Add the flour, salt, red pepper, baking powder, and Old Bay. Dip the haddock fillets in the batter and deep-fry them in a heavy skillet over medium-high heat. Serve hot.

MAKES 8 SERVINGS

Meatballs

The Dutch Kitchen's homemade meatballs are served family style with country sausage and baked chicken. This banquet also includes Pennsylvania Dutch Filling (see page 111), mashed potatoes, vegetables, and, of course, the salad bar. It is a popular dinner for families who gather at the restaurant for special-occasion meals.

1	*pound ground beef*
1	*small green bell pepper, diced*
1	*small onion, chopped*
2	*eggs, well beaten*
¼	*cup grated Parmesan cheese*
½	*cup tomato sauce*
2	*teaspoons minced garlic*
2	*teaspoons salt*
1	*teaspoon black pepper*

Preheat the oven to 350°F. In a large mixing bowl combine the ground beef, green pepper, onion, eggs, Parmesan cheese, tomato sauce, garlic, salt, and pepper. Mix well with your hands. With a small ice cream scoop, form the mixture into small meatballs. Place the meatballs on a greased baking sheet and bake for 30 minutes. Serve with pasta and tomato sauce.

MAKES 1 DOZEN MEATBALLS

Breaded Center Cut Pork Chops

F ew entrées are as handsome, or as satisfying as a pair of thick, center-cut pork chops, especially if they are accompanied on their plate by a baked apple and a mound of tangy slaw.

1½   cups plain breadcrumbs

1   teaspoon garlic salt

½   teaspoon black pepper

½   teaspoon paprika

1   teaspoon dried parsley flakes

1   cup milk

6   (4-ounce) center cut chops

Preheat the oven to 425°F. In a medium mixing bowl blend together the breadcrumbs, garlic salt, black pepper, paprika, and parsley flakes. Dip each chop into the milk, and then lightly toss the chop into the breading until coated. Place the chops on a baking sheet and bake for 12 to 15 minutes. When finished, the chops should have a golden brown appearance. These go well with the Baked Apples (see page 115).

MAKES 6 SERVINGS

Simple Beef Eye Roast

Sunday supper supreme. The Levkulics start with a partially frozen roast as a way of insuring that the interior can be juicy-rare while the outside gets a nice dark crust. Horseradish sauce is an essential companion.

1	*(4- to 6-pound) partially frozen beef rib-eye roast*
¾	*teaspoon salt*
¼	*teaspoon fresh ground black pepper*
½	*cup water*

Preheat the oven to broil. Place the beef on a rack in a shallow roasting pan and season it with the salt and pepper. Broil the beef uncovered for 6 to 8 minutes in order to sear the sides. Remove from the broiler and turn the oven to bake at 300°F. Add water to the roasting pan, cover it, and place it in the oven to bake for 1½ to 2½ hours to reach an internal temperature of 160°F for medium. When done, let it stand for 15 minutes before carving. Serve warm accompanied with either our Hot or Cold Horseradish Sauce (see page 38).

MAKES 12 TO 14 SERVINGS

Pineapple Glazed Smoked Ham

Ham is a pillar of Pennsylvania cookery, from the chip-chopped ham sandwich of Pittsburgh to the beautiful smoked hams of Lancaster County. This recipe is the classical way with ham steaks, enrobed in fruity sweet glaze.

1	(10-pound) smoked ham
1	cup light brown sugar
½	cup honey
1	tablespoon Dijon mustard
8	ounces lemon-lime soda
1	cup pineapple juice
1½	cups orange juice
¼	teaspoon cloves

Preheat the oven to 300°F and bake the ham in a Dutch oven for 3 hours.

Combine the brown sugar, honey, Dijon mustard, lemon-lime soda, pineapple juice, orange juice, and cloves in a large bowl. After cooking for 3 hours baste the ham with the glaze and bake for an additional 30 minutes.

MAKES 8 TO 10 SERVINGS

· SWEETS ·

A Perfect Single Piecrust

Mud Pie

Classic Raisin Pie

Deep Dish
Caramel Apple Pie

Pumpkin Pie

Montgomery Pie

Lemon Sponge Pie

Shoo Fly Pie

Shoo Fly Cake

Chocolate Fudge Cake

Toasted Pound Cake

Angel Food Cake

Coconut Cake

Banana Cake

Seven Minute Frosting

Creamy Peanut
Butter Icing

Applesauce Cake

Cheesecake

Jewish Apple Cake

Raisin Cake

Tapioca Pudding

Rice Pudding

Bread Pudding
with Vanilla Sauce

Blueberry Bread Pudding

Blueberry Cobbler

Monster Cookies

Cut-Out Sugar Cookies

PA Dutch
Soft Sugar Cookies

Feather Light Donuts

A Perfect Single Piecrust

The key to this simple piecrust is not to over handle the dough. It's great not only for Shoo Fly Pie, but for any fruit pie or even a savory turkey pie.

1⅓   cups sifted all-purpose flour

½   teaspoon salt

½   cup vegetable shortening

3   tablespoons cold water

Preheat the oven to 425°F. Combine the flour and salt in a large mixing bowl. Cut in the vegetable shortening until the mixture resembles coarse crumbs. Sprinkle the cold water over the crumbs and quickly toss with a fork until just combined. Mold the dough into a ball; do not over handle. Roll the dough out onto a floured surface. Place it into a greased 9-inch pie pan. Line the top of the dough with aluminum foil and fill the pie shell with uncooked beans. The weight helps prevent bubbling. Bake the piecrust for 15 to 20 minutes.

MAKES 1 PIECRUST

Mud Pie

Here's a pie with a little bit of everything and a lot of big-chunk Oreo cookies. Before it is served at the restaurant, the waitress tops each piece with syrup, nuts, and whipped cream.

1	cup peanut butter
1	frozen chocolate 9-inch pie shell
3	cups vanilla ice cream, softened
1	cup chocolate syrup
1	cup chopped peanuts
2	cups crushed Oreo cookies
3	cups chocolate ice cream, softened
	Whipped cream for topping
	Peanuts for topping
	Chocolate syrup for topping

Spread the peanut butter over the bottom of the chocolate pie shell. Add the vanilla ice cream and spread to a smooth layer. Drizzle the chocolate syrup, peanuts, and Oreos over the vanilla ice cream. Spread the chocolate ice cream on top. Lightly press down the ice cream into the pie shell. Wrap the pie in plastic wrap and freeze for 1 hour. Serve the pie topped with whipped cream, peanuts, and chocolate syrup.

MAKES 8 SERVINGS

Classic Raisin Pie

Some Pennsylvania Dutch cooks refer to this pie as "funeral pie" because that was the traditional occasion on which to serve it. At the Dutch Kitchen, it's especially popular around Thanksgiving.

2	cups raisins
1	cup orange juice
1	cup water
½	cup plus 1 tablespoon sugar
2	tablespoons cornstarch
1	teaspoon allspice
½	cup chopped walnuts
1	tablespoon lemon juice
2	(9-inch) unbaked piecrusts
1	egg, beaten

In a saucepan combine the raisins, orange juice, and water. Bring the mixture to a boil. Reduce the heat and simmer for 5 minutes. In a bowl combine ½ cup of the sugar, cornstarch, and allspice. Stir the sugar mixture into the raisin mixture. Cook and stir over medium heat until thickened, approximately 1 minute. Remove the pan from the heat and stir in the walnuts and lemon juice. Let the batter cool for 10 minutes. Preheat the oven to 425°F. Pour the batter into one piecrust. Cover the pie with the second piecrust. Cut slits in the top piecrust to release steam. Brush the top crust with the egg and sprinkle the remaining 1 tablespoon of sugar over the crust. Bake the pie for about 10 minutes. Reduce the heat to 365°F and continue baking for 25 to 30 minutes or until the filling is bubbly and the crust is golden. Let the pie cool for 30 minutes before serving.

MAKES 12 SERVINGS

COAL CANDY

Christmas tradition says that boys and girls who have been naughty get a lump of coal in their stocking rather than a fun toy or a sweet treat. But in the mining towns of Pennsylvania, coal would never be used to signify bad behavior. Here, coal is a good thing, and children are delighted to find lumps of coal in their Christmas stocking. *Coal candy*, that is.

At the cash register in the old diner section of the Dutch Kitchen, you can buy locally-made coal candy by the bucketful. It is licorice, black and shiny like a nugget of freshly-mined anthracite. It comes in large, irregular chunks packaged with a small hammer. The way to enjoy it is to set a hunk out on a clean surface and use the hammer to smash it into little bite-size fragments.

The unique confection was invented over in the neighboring town of Pottsville, where Ned Buckley's family has been running the Mootz Candy store on Main Street since 1908. Mootz is known for chocolate-covered nuts, creamy peanut rolls, molasses-coconut strips, and chocolate novelties made in molds that look like hairdresser tools, golf clubs, antique cars, and bingo boards. It was Ned Buckley's grandmother who came up with the idea for coal candy some time in the 1950s when the coal industry was still thriving. Mootz sells its coal candy, known as Black Diamonds, in boxes, miniature miner's buckets, and toy train cars. And at Christmas, you can buy stockings already filled with it.

Deep Dish Caramel Apple Pie

Tom suggests that Caramel Apple Pie is an especially fitting dessert in the autumn. He says it reminds him of the caramel apples enjoyed each year by visitors to the Bloomsburg Fair, a Columbia County tradition since 1855.

2	*unbaked piecrusts (see page 173)*
6	*to 8 medium apples*
2	*teaspoons ground cinnamon*
½	*cup sugar*
¼	*teaspoon ground nutmeg*
2	*tablespoons chilled butter, chopped into pieces*
1	*tablespoon milk*
1	*(16-ounce) jar caramel sauce*
½	*gallon vanilla ice cream*
1	*(16-ounce) can whipped cream*

Preheat the oven to 375°F. Place 1 unbaked piecrust in a greased pie plate or tin. Peel, core, and slice the apples. Place them in a large mixing bowl. Add the cinnamon, sugar, nutmeg, and butter. Toss this mixture to blend. Put the apple mixture into the piecrust. Place the other piecrust on top of the apples and pinch the edges. Brush the top crust with the milk. Bake the pie for 1 hour. When the pie has finished baking and cools for 10 minutes, serve each slice in a deep dessert dish topped with warm caramel sauce, ice cream, and whipped cream.

MAKES 12 SERVINGS

Pumpkin Pie

Pumpkin pie is served at the Dutch Kitchen from September through December. Our favorite recipe includes not only autumn pumpkin, but also honey from Tom's hives and dark Dutch molasses.

1½	cups cooked pumpkin
2	eggs
⅔	cup brown sugar
¼	cup honey
1	tablespoon molasses
½	teaspoon salt
1	tablespoon cornstarch
¼	teaspoon ginger
¼	teaspoon cloves
1	teaspoon ground cinnamon
1½	cups scalded milk
1	unbaked piecrust, (see page 173)

Preheat the oven to 425°F. Strain the pumpkin through a sieve. Place the pumpkin in a large mixing bowl. Separate the eggs, reserving the whites. Beat the egg yolks and add them to the pumpkin along with the brown sugar, honey, molasses, salt, cornstarch, ginger, cloves, and cinnamon. Gradually add the scalded milk and mix well. With an electric mixer beat the egg whites until stiff and fold them into the pumpkin mixture. Pour the pumpkin mixture into the unbaked piecrust. Bake for 10 minutes. Reduce the heat to 350°F and continue to bake for 30 minutes longer.

MAKES 12 SERVINGS

Montgomery Pie

A country-kitchen legend, Montgomery pie is basically shoo fly pie but with the zest of fresh lemon.

PIE:

½	cup molasses
½	cup sugar
1	egg
1	cup water
2	tablespoons all-purpose flour
	Juice of 1 lemon
1	teaspoon lemon zest
1	unbaked piecrust (see page 173)

TOPPING:

¼	cup (½ stick) butter
⅔	cup sugar
1	egg, well beaten
½	cup buttermilk
½	teaspoon baking soda
1¼	cups all-purpose flour

For the pie, combine the molasses, sugar, egg, water, flour, lemon juice, and lemon zest in a bowl. Pour the mixture into the unbaked piecrust. Preheat the oven to 375°F.

For the topping, cream together the butter and sugar in a mixing bowl. Add the egg and beat thoroughly. Add the buttermilk. Sift together the baking soda and flour and add to the egg mixture. Spread the topping on top of the pie. Bake for 35 to 40 minutes.

MAKES 12 SERVINGS

Lemon Sponge Pie

Light and fluffy, this is a refreshing pie that is an especially welcome dessert after a full-flavored meal.

2	*tablespoons butter*
1½	*cups sugar*
3	*eggs, separated*
3	*tablespoons all-purpose flour*
½	*teaspoon salt*
	Juice of 1 lemon
1	*teaspoon lemon zest*
1½	*cups warm milk*
1	*unbaked piecrust (see page 173)*

Preheat the oven to 350°F. Cream together the butter and sugar in a mixing bowl. Add the egg yolks and beat well. Add the flour, salt, lemon juice, lemon zest, and warm milk. In a separate mixing bowl beat the egg whites until stiff. Fold them into the batter. Pour the batter into the unbaked piecrust. Bake for 45 minutes. Serve warm or chilled.

MAKES 12 SERVINGS

Shoo Fly Pie

A signature dish of Pennsylvania Dutch country, Shoo Fly Pie is on the menu every day at the Dutch Kitchen. The oddest account for its name that we've ever seen says that the crumbly texture of the pie's top resembles a cauliflower, which in French is *choufleur*. Like so many words in the Dutch vernacular *choufleur* somehow got corrupted to *shoo fly*. A more likely explanation is that cooks traditionally cool it on a windowsill, where its super-sweet aroma will attract flies . . . not to mention any hungry human strolling past.

1½	cups all-purpose flour
¼	teaspoon salt
1	cup packed brown sugar
¼	cup vegetable shortening
¼	teaspoon baking soda
½	cup hot water
½	cup molasses
1	(8-inch) unbaked piecrust (see page 173)

Preheat the oven to 450°F. In a mixing bowl combine the flour, salt, brown sugar, and shortening and mix with your hands until the mixture resembles coarse crumbs. In a separate bowl combine the baking soda, hot water, and molasses. Add all but 1 cup of the crumbs to the molasses mixture and gently stir. Pour the combined mixture into the piecrust. Sprinkle the pie with the remaining 1 cup crumbs. Bake the pie for 10 minutes.

MAKES 10 TO 12 SERVINGS

Shoo Fly Cake

Shoo Fly Cake is similar to what some local cooks call "dry bottom" shoo fly pie: the same basic ingredients, but without the gooey, moist ribbon in the center. It's an excellent recipe to have on hand when you're in a hurry: No crust required.

1	cup shortening
4	cups all-purpose flour
2	cups sugar
1	cup mild molasses
2	cups hot water
2	teaspoons baking soda

Preheat the oven to 375°F. In a large bowl mix together the shortening, flour, and sugar with your hands until the mixture forms coarse crumbs. Reserve 1 cup of this mixture to be used later. In a separate bowl mix together the molasses, hot water, and baking soda. Add the wet mixture to the dry mixture. Pour the filling into a greased and floured 9 x 13-inch baking pan. Sprinkle the reserved 1 cup crumb mixture on top. Bake for 10 minutes. Reduce the heat to 350°F and bake for 40 more minutes.

MAKES 12 SERVINGS

Chocolate Fudge Cake

This recipe comes from Jennifer Levkulic's great-grandmother Edith, who was the head baker at Schuylkill County's Necho Allen Hotel. It is essential to use a cup of already-brewed coffee, not coffee grounds.

2	cups all-purpose flour
2	cups sugar
2	teaspoons baking soda
1	teaspoon baking powder
¾	cup cocoa
1	cup milk
1	cup coffee
½	cup canola oil
2	eggs
	Creamy Peanut Butter Icing (see page 189)

Preheat the oven to 350°F. Mix together the flour, sugar, baking soda, baking powder, cocoa, milk, coffee, canola oil, and eggs in a large bowl. Pour the batter into two greased and floured 9-inch-round, cake pans. Bake the cakes for 30 minutes. Once the cakes are done, let them cool. Spread the icing between the layers and over the top and sides of the cooled cake.

MAKES 12 SERVINGS

Toasted Pound Cake

Jennifer describes this old-fashioned dessert as one that evokes memories of the drug store lunch counter. "We like to use Leiby's vanilla ice cream," she says. It is made locally in the town of Tamaqua.

CAKE:

6   eggs

1   cup (2 sticks) butter

1   pound confectioners' sugar

2½   cups all-purpose flour

3   teaspoons baking powder

½   cup milk

TOPPING:

    Vanilla ice cream

    Hot fudge

Preheat the oven to 350°F. Separate the egg whites from the yolks. Beat the egg whites in a bowl and set aside. In a separate bowl, cream the butter, sugar, and egg yolks. Add the flour, baking powder, and milk. Beat the mixture for 10 minutes. Fold in the egg whites and pour into a greased Bundt pan. Bake for 1 hour. Let the cake cool. Slice the pound cake in 2-inch slices and toast. Top the slices with the vanilla ice cream and hot fudge to serve.

MAKES 12 SERVINGS

Angel Food Cake

Michelle Morgan gets credit for this truly angelic cake that is so light you can always have a slice . . . or, if you are her husband, John Morgan, two slices. It's especially good topped with seasonal fruits.

1¾   cups egg whites (12 to 14 eggs)

1¼   cups cake flour

¾   plus 1 cups sugar

½   teaspoon salt

1½   teaspoons cream of tartar

1   teaspoon vanilla extract

½   teaspoon almond extract

Separate your eggs while still cold and let the egg whites sit at room temperature for 1 hour. In a large bowl sift the flour once to measure. Sift the flour again with ¾ cup of the sugar. Sift the flour and sugar 3 more times. Preheat the oven to 375°F. In a separate bowl beat the egg whites, salt, and cream of tartar with an electric mixer on medium speed until stiff peaks form. On high speed beat in the remaining 1 cup sugar, ¼ cup at a time, until stiff peaks form. Fold in the extracts. Sprinkle the flour mixture, ¼ cup at a time, over the beaten egg whites gently folding the flour into the egg whites with a whisk after each addition. Be careful not to overbeat the batter. Push the batter into an ungreased Bundt pan. Cut through the batter with a knife 2 times to remove any bubbles. Even out the top. Bake the cake on the lowest oven rack for 30 minutes.

MAKES 12 SERVINGS

Coconut Cake

Regulars count on the Dutch Kitchen being open for Easter, and one of the dishes that is available that Sunday is this especially angelic cake. Customers Mr. Holt and his daughter Barbara asked Jennifer if she could make it throughout the rest of the year as well.

2	cups sugar
½	cup (1 stick) butter
3	eggs, separated
2	cups cake flour
2	teaspoons baking powder
1	cup milk
1	(16-ounce) bag sweetened coconut
	Seven Minute Frosting (see page 188)

Preheat the oven to 350°F. Cream the sugar and butter in a mixing bowl. Add the egg yolks and mix. Sift the flour and baking powder together and add the flour mixture and milk alternately to the egg yolk mixture. Mix in the coconut. In a small bowl beat the egg whites and fold them into the batter. Gently pour the batter into two 9-inch, greased and floured cake pans. Bake the cake for 35 minutes. Top with Seven Minute Frosting.

MAKES 12 SERVINGS

Banana Cake

Traditionally, the Dutch Kitchen made banana cake in a bread pan, like zucchini bread. But recently the cooks discovered how wonderful it is to turn the same recipe into a layer cake topped with peanut butter icing with fresh sliced bananas between the layers.

2	cups sugar
1	cup (2 sticks) butter
4	eggs
2	teaspoons baking soda
1	teaspoon baking powder
¼	teaspoon salt
3	cups all-purpose flour
1	cup sour cream
2	cups mashed ripe bananas
2	teaspoons vanilla extract

Preheat the oven to 350°F. Cream together the sugar and butter in a mixing bowl. Add the eggs and beat well. Mix in the baking soda, baking powder, salt, flour, sour cream, bananas, and vanilla. Pour the batter into a greased and floured 9 x 13-inch baking pan. Bake for 10 minutes. Reduce the heat to 300°F and bake for an additional 45 minutes.

MAKES 12 SERVINGS

Seven Minute Frosting

This fluffy frosting is the perfect complement to coconut cake.

---

2   egg whites, unbeaten

1½   cups sugar

5   tablespoons cold water

¼   teaspoon cream of tartar

1   teaspoon vanilla extract

In a double boiler over high heat combine the egg whites, sugar, cold water, and cream of tartar. Beat the ingredients constantly with a wire whisk for 7 minutes. Remove from the heat. Add the vanilla and pour the mixture into a glass bowl. Using an electric mixer continue to mix until the frosting is very fluffy and resembles marshmallow fluff.

MAKES FROSTING FOR 1 (9-INCH) LAYER CAKE

Creamy Peanut Butter Icing

A perfect mantle for the Chocolate Fudge Cake (see page 183), this icing is especially welcome when you make the Banana Cake (see page 187) and use it with sliced bananas between the layers.

5	cups confectioners' sugar
1	cup peanut butter
½	cup (1 stick) butter, at room temperature
½	cup milk
1	teaspoon vanilla extract

In a mixing bowl beat the sugar, peanut butter, butter, milk, and vanilla together with a mixer until smooth and creamy. Spread over the cake.

MAKES 7 CUPS

Applesauce Cake

Jennifer Levkulic's great-grandmother, a baker and restaurateur, passed along this treasured recipe, which has been a lifelong delight of Jen's . . . and a favorite of those Dutch Kitchen customers lucky enough to nab a piece when it's available.

2	cups all-purpose flour
1	cup sugar
1	teaspoon salt
1	teaspoon ground cinnamon
½	teaspoon ground nutmeg
¼	teaspoon cloves
2	teaspoons baking soda
1	cup raisins
1	cup chopped walnuts
½	cup (1 stick) melted butter
2	cups applesauce.

Preheat the oven to 350°F. Sift together the flour, sugar, salt, cinnamon, nutmeg, cloves, and baking soda in a large bowl. Add the raisins, walnuts, butter, and applesauce. Pour the batter into a greased and floured 9 x 13-inch baking pan. Bake the cake for about 45 minutes.

MAKES 12 SERVINGS

Cheesecake

There's nothing fancy or baroque about this cheesecake, which is for the confectionery purist. It is creamy, smooth, and simple.

1	(8-ounce) package cream cheese, softened
2	tablespoons butter
½	cup sugar
1	egg
2	tablespoons all-purpose flour
½	cup milk
2	tablespoons lemon juice
1	(9-inch) graham cracker crust, unbaked

Preheat the oven to 350°F. In a large bowl mix together the cream cheese and butter. Add the sugar and egg and beat until creamy. Add the flour and milk and beat until smooth. Stir in the lemon juice. Pour the mixture into the graham cracker crust. Bake the cheesecake for 35 minutes.

MAKES 12 SERVINGS

Jewish Apple Cake

We've never seen Jewish Apple Cake anywhere outside of Frackville, and no one we know has a good explanation of how it came to be a local specialty. Whatever its history, there is no denying its popularity. Tom Levkulic says, "When we put this cake out, it usually disappears within an hour—proof that cook Billy Rumbel's hard work pays off."

4	eggs
1	cup canola oil
½	cup orange juice
3	cups unsifted all-purpose flour
2	cups plus ½ cup sugar
1	teaspoon baking powder
2½	teaspoons vanilla extract
8	apples, peeled and cored
2	teaspoons ground cinnamon

Preheat the oven to 350°F. Beat the eggs in a mixing bowl. Mix in the oil and orange juice. Add the flour, 2 cups of the sugar, and baking powder. Add the vanilla. Cut the apples into slices. Combine the apple slices with the cinnamon and the remaining ½ cup sugar. Pour half the batter into a greased Bundt pan. Layer the apple mixture on top of the batter and top with the remaining batter. Bake for 1½ hours.

MAKES 12 SERVINGS

Raisin Cake

Raisins are popular in many Pennsylvania Dutch desserts because they keep well and can be used in cakes and pies year around. This cake is a longtime regional favorite—no icing needed, just a dusting of powdered sugar before serving.

1	pound raisins
1	cup (2 sticks) butter
1	pound brown sugar
2	teaspoons baking soda
¼	cup warm water
4	cups all-purpose flour
2	teaspoon ground cinnamon
1	teaspoon ground nutmeg
1	cup applesauce
1	cup chopped walnuts

In a saucepan cook the raisins in 2½ cups boiling water for 10 minutes; drain. Preheat the oven to 350°F. Add the butter and sugar to the raisins. Dissolve the baking soda in the warm water in a small bowl. When the raisins cool add the dissolved baking soda. Add the flour, cinnamon, nutmeg, applesauce, and walnuts. Pour into a greased and floured 9 x 13-inch baking pan. Bake the cake for 1 hour.

MAKES 12 SERVINGS

Tapioca Pudding

Aficionados of diner lingo know Tapioca as "cat's eye" pudding; and no self-respecting diner menu is complete without it. Serve it slightly warm with maybe a dab of whipped cream on top.

1	egg
2	tablespoons tapioca
¼	cup sugar
¼	teaspoon salt
2	cups milk
½	teaspoon vanilla extract

Break the egg into a saucepan over medium heat and gently stir. Add the tapioca, sugar, salt, and milk. Cook until the mixture boils and the tapioca softens. Remove from heat and let the pudding stand for 15 minutes and then stir in the vanilla. Serve warm or at room temperature.

MAKES 6 SERVINGS

Rice Pudding

What would a diner be without good rice pudding? This super creamy recipe from Jen's great-grandmother has been on the menu since opening day.

3	eggs
½	cup sugar
6	cups milk
1½	cups rice
2	teaspoons vanilla extract

Beat the eggs and sugar together in a saucepan until smooth. Add the milk and rice. Cook the mixture on medium heat until thick and the rice floats on top. Add the vanilla. Remove the pan from the heat and allow the mixture to cool.

MAKES 6 SERVINGS

Bread Pudding with Vanilla Sauce

It is not unusual for a serious Pennsylvania Dutch meal to begin with a goodly taste of dessert; and so for many years, this bread pudding was offered at the salad bar with other sweet things. Now it is most often served warm as an after-meal dessert, topped with a secret-recipe vanilla sauce.

6	eggs
3	cups half-and-half
2	cups sugar
2	teaspoons vanilla extract
1	teaspoon ground cinnamon
1	teaspoon ground nutmeg
1	crusty loaf white bread, cubed
	Vanilla ice cream, softened

Preheat the oven to 325°F. In a bowl beat the eggs well. Add the half-and-half, sugar, vanilla, cinnamon, and nutmeg and mix well. Put the bread cubes into a large bowl. Pour the egg mixture over the bread cubes and lightly mix. Pour the bread mixture into a greased 9 x 13-inch baking pan. Bake for 35 minutes or until the top is lightly browned. Remove from the oven and serve warm. Drizzle the ice cream over each individual serving.

MAKES 12 SERVINGS

Blueberry Bread Pudding

This is a traditional bread pudding with one wonderful difference—a pint of blueberries. Needless to say, the time you want to make it is in the summer when farm-fresh berries are ripe and sweet.

1	loaf stale white sandwich bread
4	eggs, well beaten
2	teaspoons vanilla extract
3	cups milk
½	teaspoon ground cinnamon
2	cups blueberries
½	cup packed brown sugar
½	cup (1 stick) chilled butter

Preheat the oven to 300°F. Cut the bread into 2-inch pieces. In a large mixing bowl combine the eggs, vanilla, milk, and cinnamon. Mix well and add the bread pieces. Fold in the blueberries. Place the pudding into a greased 9 x 13-inch baking pan. In a separate small bowl combine the brown sugar and butter. Rub this mixture together with your fingers until it becomes crumb-like. Sprinkle over the bread pudding. Place the baking pan in a water bath by placing the pan in a larger pan that is filled one-fourth full with water. Place the pans in the oven and bake for 1½ hours or until a butter knife comes out clean.

MAKES 12 SERVINGS

Blueberry Cobbler

Tom Levkulic's mom used to make this recipe using fresh Pennsylvania Pocono Mountain blueberries from the Smiths' farm. While it makes a fine dessert after supper, it's in the Pennsylvania Dutch tradition to serve such sweets with every meal, including breakfast.

2	cups fresh blueberries
3	tablespoons butter
¾	plus 1 cups sugar
1	teaspoon baking powder
¼	teaspoon salt
½	cup milk
1	cup all-purpose flour
1	tablespoon cornstarch
⅔	cup boiling water

Preheat the oven to 375°F. Cover the bottom of an 8-inch-square pan with the blueberries. In a large bowl mix together the butter, ¾ cup of the sugar, baking powder, salt, milk, and flour until crumbly. Pour the batter over the berries. In a separate bowl mix together the remaining 1 cup sugar and the cornstarch and sprinkle the mixture over the batter. Pour the boiling water over the top. Bake the cobbler for 45 minutes.

MAKES 12 SERVINGS

Monster Cookies

As soon as you see one, it's no secret how these cookies get their name. They are monster-size and packed with gobs of goodies.

½	cup (1 stick) butter
1¼	cups firmly packed brown sugar
1	cup granulated sugar
3	eggs
1⅓	cups peanut butter
2	teaspoons baking soda
4½	cups oatmeal
⅔	cup M&Ms
⅔	cup chocolate chips
2	tablespoons vanilla extract
½	cup chopped walnuts

Preheat the oven to 350°F. Cream together the butter and both sugars. Beat in the eggs. Stir in the peanut butter, baking soda, oatmeal, M&Ms, chocolate chips, vanilla, and walnuts. Place ⅓ cup scoops of cookie batter onto an ungreased cookie sheet. Bake the cookies for 15 to 20 minutes.

MAKES 1 DOZEN COOKIES

Cut-Out Sugar Cookies

At the Dutch Kitchen's Christmas time Make-A-Wish celebration, star sugar cookies are given to every child at the Breakfast with Santa festivities.

1	teaspoon baking soda
2	teaspoons warm water
2	cups (4 sticks) butter at room temperature
2¼	cups sugar
6	eggs
8	cups all-purpose flour
1	teaspoon cream of tartar

Dissolve the baking soda in the warm water; set aside. With an electric mixer cream the butter and sugar together in a mixing bowl. Add the eggs and beat well. In a separate bowl combine the flour, dissolved baking soda mix, and cream of tarter. Add the butter mixture to the flour mixture and mix with your hands until the dough is not too sticky. Divide the dough into 6 balls. Roll each ball lightly in flour. Cover each dough ball with plastic wrap and refrigerate for 1 hour.

When ready to bake, preheat the oven to 350°F. Roll out 1 ball at a time onto a floured surface with a rolling pin. Cut the dough into desired shapes and bake the cookies for 8 minutes.

MAKES 6 DOZEN COOKIES

Note: Each ball makes 1 dozen cookies. The balls can be frozen and used at later date.

PA Dutch Soft Sugar Cookies

You will always find soft sugar cookies arrayed on the counter in the Dutch Kitchen diner car. Dunk them in coffee or eat them plain. The recipe is one for which Tom and Jen searched high and low, finally securing it from a friend next door named Barbara.

1	cup (2 sticks) butter
3	cups sugar
4	eggs
2	teaspoons vanilla extract
6	cups all-purpose flour
2	teaspoons salt
1	teaspoon baking soda
1	teaspoon baking powder
2	cups sour cream
	Cinnamon-sugar

Preheat the oven to 375°F. Cream the butter and sugar in a bowl. Beat in the eggs and add the vanilla. Add the flour, salt, baking soda, baking powder, and sour cream. With a mini ice cream scoop, place the dough onto a greased cookie sheet. Sprinkle the top of the unbaked cookies with cinnamon-sugar just before baking. Bake the cookies for 10 to 12 minutes.

MAKES 2 DOZEN COOKIES

Note: The cookies bake higher if mixed by hand and if the eggs, sour cream, and butter are cold.

201

Feather Light Donuts

The regular morning crew at the Dutch Kitchen, which includes employees and their families as well as customers, count on these donuts made fresh every day.

4	(¼-ounce) packages active dry yeast
3	cups warm milk
2	cups cold mashed potatoes
½	plus 2½ cups sugar
1	cup vegetable oil
4	teaspoons salt
4	teaspoons vanilla extract
1	teaspoon baking soda
1	teaspoon baking powder
4	eggs
11	cups all-purpose flour
1	teaspoon ground cinnamon

In a large mixing bowl dissolve the yeast in the warm milk. Add the potatoes, ½ cup of the sugar, oil, salt, vanilla, baking soda, baking powder, and eggs. Mix well. Add enough of the flour to form a soft dough, mixing with your hands. Place the dough in a greased bowl, turning to grease the dough. Cover the bowl with a towel and set aside in a warm area until doubled in size, about 1 hour. Punch the dough down. Place it on a floured surface and roll it to ½-inch thickness. Cut the dough into donuts. Place the donuts onto a greased cookie sheet and let them double in size, about 45 minutes. Heat a deep fryer to 350°F and fry the donuts until golden. Drain on paper towels.

MAKES 2 DOZEN DONUTS

INDEX

Italics numbers refer to pages with illustrations.